THE TRUTH ABOUT
ABOUT

BRANDS

Brian D. Till and Donna Heckler

PEARSON

Prentice Hall

Harlow, England • London • New York • Boston • San Francisco • Toronto
Sydney • Tokyo • Singapore • Hong Kong • Seoul • Taipei • New Delhi
Cape Town • Madrid • Mexico City • Amsterdam • Munich • Paris • Milan

PEARSON EDUCATION LIMITED

Edinburgh Gate
Harlow CM20 2JE
Tel: +44 (0)1279 623623
Fax: +44 (0)1279 431059
Website: www.pearsoned.co.uk

First published in Great Britain 2008

© Pearson Education Limited 2008

The rights of Brian D. Till and Donna Heckler to be identified as authors of this work have been asserted by them in accordance with the Copyright, Designs and Patents Act 1988.

ISBN: 978-0-273-72075-1

British Library Cataloguing-in-Publication Data
A catalogue record for this book is available from the British Library

Original edition, entitled TRUTH ABOUT CREATING BRANDS PEOPLE LOVE, THE, by TILL, BRIAN D. AND HECKLER, DONNA, published by Pearson Education, Inc, publishing as FT PRESS, Copyright © 2008.

This edition published by PEARSON EDUCATION LTD, Copyright © 2008.

This edition is manufactured in Great Britain and is authorised for sale only in UK, EUROPE, MIDDLE EAST AND AFRICA.

10 9 8 7 6 5 4 3 2 1
12 11 10 09 08

Printed and bound in Great Britain by Ashford Colour Press Ltd, Gosport

The publisher's policy is to use paper manufactured from sustainable forests.

From Brian D. Till:

I dedicate this book to my family –
my parents Lee and Nancy Till and my brother Ken –
for a lifetime of love and encouragement,
and also to my close friends who have immensely
enriched the quality of my life.

From Donna Heckler:

For all their support, encouragement and love,
I dedicate this book to my family –
my parents Al and Gerry Heckler and my sisters Karen
Thompson and Jennifer Burran.
I dedicate this book to my close friends whose
love and support I truly cherish.
Importantly, I dedicate this book to the children in my life –
Andy, Nick, Leah, Fiona and Audrey –
you always help me to realise what truly matters in life.

Preface

Creating brands people love seems so easy. Just look around at all the wonderful brands that we experience every day. Yet, creating brands people love requires more than simply love of a product and spectacularly creative advertising – it requires intelligent, strategic and coordinated decisions in many areas of marketing. Packaging, promotion, advertising, positioning, distribution and pricing are just some of the important functions that, when successfully managed, lead to profitable brands that matter to consumers.

The purpose of this book is to illustrate universal truths about brand management that cover the range of brand-building activities. These truths transcend context, providing important insight irrespective of industry-specific dynamics. The guidelines here are as relevant to a marketing manager for a steel producer as for a cereal maker; as meaningful to a brand manager for coffee machines as for a ski resort; as useful to someone running an art gallery as to someone managing a high-end hotel.

For experienced and well-trained marketing managers, these truths provide a touchstone to those basic principles that are sometimes overlooked in day-to-day decision making. For the up-and-coming brand manager, this book provides thoughtful guidance that will serve you well over the course of a career. For senior executives responsible for the marketing function but not formally trained, the book serves as a framework to think about brand building and from which to challenge your marketing staff. Finally, for students, you will find these truths to be a solid foundation for life-long learning in this fascinating business.

The following chapters cover an assortment of issues regularly faced by marketing and brand managers such as media, brand extensions, brand names, use of celebrities, packaging and so on. Importantly, though, none of those decisions will matter unless your basic product or service offering is on target. The product or service itself is the starting foundation of a great brand.

Consider Honda. Certainly there are cars more luxurious, cars that deliver greater thrills and cars that are more stylish. But Honda nails the essence of a great product – reliability, excellent build quality, comfortable, well-planned ergonomics and good fuel economy. Although Honda's brand image is not flashy, Honda's image does have appeal to a significant group of people. Importantly, the starting point for Honda as a brand is Honda the product.

Gas station and convenience store QuickTrip is another good example of a brand that pays close attention to the little things. The cashiers, in addition to their speedy service, are quick with a "Many thanks" or "Come back and see us soon". The consistency from QuickTrip is not simple coincidence but rather an intentional focus on speed and pleasantness. At many service stations, when filling to an automatic preset of $20, the rate of fuel flow drops to a trickle at $19.80 or so, and then the last twenty cents worth dribbles in. Not at QuickTrip. The gas flow is constantly strong until it hits exactly $20. A small detail indeed, but a detail that reinforces the promise embodied in their name – quick trip.

Without diminishing the role and importance of public relations, creative TV advertising, an engaging website, captivating packaging, motivating promotions, or any of the other tools that collectively build strong brands and drive profitability, there is tremendous importance in putting first things first – and the first thing is a fundamentally great product. Great products make great brands.

The Truth About Brands is a complete toolbox of ideas, strategies and techniques that can take a great product and transform it into a profitable brand people will love. Each concept has at its core a focus on how to connect with the consumer in a meaningful way. Be empowered, challenge conventional wisdom, think strategically, and use this book as a guide to creating a bond between your customers and your brand.

1

Managing brands is not common sense

If common sense is what most people naturally use in the absence of education and training, then effective brand management is not common sense.

Certainly the more features and benefits you highlight about your brand, the more attractive the brand will be. The more people you try to appeal to, the more effective your advertising will be. That market share is the most important measure of a brand's success is obvious. And what name you attach to a brand isn't all that important – it's what the brand actually does for the consumer that makes the difference. It is completely obvious that "quality" is an effective marketing message. Brand extension as the best way to introduce a new product seems apparent.

Every one of the preceding statements is either partially or completely false.

Yet, talk to many who claim to be marketers, and they will espouse the validity of these statements. Dig a little deeper, and you will find that their marketing "expertise" is based on their idea of common sense. The difficulty with divining marketing strategy is that people live and breathe marketing every day as consumers. People see advertising. People open packages. People try new products. People participate in promotions. In the course of being consumers, people form opinions about what works, or doesn't work, based on their preferences. Their experience as consumers leads them to believe that marketing is basic common sense.

More often than not, effective brand development is the complete opposite of common sense. But the strong belief in this myth perpetuates bad marketing strategy. There are many instances in which administrative assistants, engineers, salespeople and so on get moved into significant marketing positions because they are "good with people"; after all, brand management is pretty much just common sense!

How many companies further reinforce this concept by making a marketing position something that their star performers must work through to advance in a corporation? Many companies do not hire marketers; instead, they rotate their sales stars or their finance prodigies through marketing for the experience. After all, since managing brands is common sense, you don't need any special expertise in it, right?

With one company, the marketing department wanted to become more creative. The department had become stale. There were no new ideas or creative solutions being offered by the department or by the agencies supporting the business. Digging a bit deeper, management discovered that the marketing department was composed primarily of salespeople. The marketing programmes developed were actually trade promotions. The advertising had become a mess, with each ad bearing multiple messages about the various product features – not a benefit to be found.

The problem this company experienced was not that there were no fresh ideas. The problem was that there was no marketing strategy. There was not a thoughtful approach to driving profitable sales from the target audience. In fact, the target audience was not even defined. Relying on common sense, the sales-oriented marketing department offered discounts and sales promotions. As good salespeople, they mentioned every feature in the ad. Unfortunately, the great common sense of the sales organisation was not enhancing the success of the business.

For senior managers, a reminder that marketing is not common sense is important. If your rise to the top was not through marketing, consider that your perspective on marketing may be based on your understanding of common sense, not marketing strategy fundamentals. Don't be like the CEO who explained that he knew all about marketing because his father had run a printing company – his idea of great marketing was when PMS colours matched. Colour match is important at some level, but surely not a driver of marketing strategy.

Effective marketing strategy and brand building are built on a foundation of principles and guidelines that run counter to our natural way of thinking. For example, building an effective brand requires not only

> More often than not, effective brand management is the opposite of common sense.

understanding what a brand stands for, but what it doesn't stand for; understanding not only who the brand is for, but who it is not for. Such exclusionary thinking is not natural – after all, it is common sense that our brand should appeal to as many people as possible.

3

TRUTH

2

No one loves your brand as much as you love it

Managing a brand is like raising a child. You nurture the brand, watch it grow, want the best for it and intervene when it is struggling. You want the brand to grow up to be strong and successful.

Just as parents find it difficult to be objective about their children, so it is with marketing managers and their brands. It is hard to see the brand from the consumer's perspective. It is difficult to appreciate the minor role the brand plays in the life of the consumer. Minor role? How is that possible? Of course, your brand is critical to your consumer; you make every effort to ensure that it is at the front of their mind. For a moment, let's not consider your brand; let's consider the life of a consumer.

US trade magazine *Ad Age* reported a few years back that the average consumer sees 6,000 brand messages a day! And, that doesn't include internet brand messaging. How is that possible? Let's think about a morning for consumers. Their Sony alarm clock goes off and they hop out of bed to climb into their Kohler shower. They wash their hair with Aveda before drying off with Ralph Lauren towels. They brush their teeth with Crest and slip into an Armani suit. They eat a few Cheerios for breakfast before jumping into their BMW to drive to the office. And you wonder why your brand is not at the front of their mind? They have barely made it through the first hour of their day!

> It is difficult to appreciate the minor role the brand plays in the life of the consumer.

To complicate matters, it is difficult to design marketing programmes that reflect your consumers', rather than your, level of involvement. Is it reasonable to expect your customers to spend thousands on a product so that they can get a free leather jacket with the brand logo emblazoned on the front? It is unreasonable to expect this if you are a consumer besieged with hundreds of brands and offers. But, if you are a brand manager, you think: Who wouldn't do whatever it takes to obtain that jacket? Is that because you, the brand manager, love your brand – or because your consumers actually love your brand?

Windex is a strong, well-known US brand that has been managed over the years by committed and enthused marketing people. Windex brand managers have dedicated a significant portion of their day-to-day life caring for this brand. But just how much do people actually care about window cleaners? How much do they really care about Windex? They may like it. They may use it. But it is simply insignificant in the scheme of their lives.

Mr or Ms Windex manager, please don't be disappointed if people leave the room during the Windex TV commercial, if they throw away the brochure you send them on "a better life through cleaner windows", or if they don't visit the Windex web page. It's not that they don't like Windex; it's just that they don't love the brand as much as you do!

Of course, the question becomes: Why does this matter to brand managers? Brand managers want cool, interesting brands. It is this desire that leads to frequent changes to a brand, changes in look, changes in advertising, changes in promotion...the list continues. Keep your brand simple and consistent. When you keep changing it because you are in love with it and you want to keep it fresh, you are forgetting this one simple principle: No one else loves your brand as much as you do.

Keep your brand simple and consistent.

TRUTH

3

The brand is not owned by marketing; everyone owns it

One of the most common mistakes in business is assuming that the brand is owned by marketing. Marketing owns the brand because they develop it through their advertising, or promotions, or logo work, or merchandising, right? Wrong. Marketing is the playmaker, creating the tactics for the brand, but every person and every department is crucial to the brand's success.

A brand is built through consistency over time. That consistency is never delivered by just one person or one team of people. Consistency is delivered by all those in the company. The experience that the sales representative provides to a customer should be consistent with the brand message. The way the CEO speaks to investors should be consistent with the brand message. Customer service operations must deliver on a brand promise. From strategic departments developing long-range plans to delivery drivers, everyone must understand and own the brand to effectively deliver its message to the market.

> The experience that the sales representative provides to a customer should be consistent with the brand message.

When Fred Smith, the founder and CEO of FedEx, appeared on Fox News he clearly articulated the "purple promise", the promise of customer service that FedEx espouses. His focus is on every one of the 280,000 employees of FedEx delivering the purple promise of the FedEx brand to every customer, every single day.

On Southwest Airlines, a singing flight attendant is part of the casual, fun Southwest experience. Do you think the brand manager called before the flight to remind the attendant to sing? No. Southwest ensures that all of its employees not only know the brand but also embrace what the brand is all about. Southwest then encourages and empowers its employees to bring the brand to life in everything they do.

Somehow, it seems easier to see how every person in a company owns a brand when it is a service brand. However, the same is true of product brands, and perhaps even more difficult to achieve because such importance is not as obvious to the employees. Let's consider BMW cars. BMW is the ultimate driving machine. Every engineer must consider that brand position when developing the next model. The sales teams will try to move a customer to a different model because of the performance available. If you take the car in for service, the service team provides the ultimate experience as well. In fact, the loan cars are planned out so that all current owners can try a new ultimate driving experience while their car is being serviced.

A basic tenet of brand building is consistency over time. When that is put into the perspective of the multitudes of employees helping to drive the brand, the importance of it can be understood. For those successful companies, brand building becomes expressed through the organisations' culture. Changing a brand message is not only about changing an ad or a logo – it is also about changing the behaviour of an organisation. Clearly, then, the most successful companies are those that have built the brand and stayed consistently true to its promise.

Consider Marriott and its capability to ensure that service is well understood by all of its employees. During the winter a few years ago, we had to take a trip to Washington DC. Horrible storms in St Louis delayed the flight. When we finally entered the DC airspace, Ronald Reagan airport was closed again because of weather. The flight landed at Baltimore/Washington International instead. Getting off the plane, a long queue formed for a taxi at what was now 1:00 a.m. Speaking to the people in front of us, we realised that we were headed to the same general area. They were on their way to a Marriott hotel in Bethesda, so we decided to go together and drop them off first. As luck would have it, as the cab pulled into the Marriott, it caught fire. (Yes, travel stories like this do happen!)

The woman behind the desk at the Marriott checked in the people from the taxi, except for us. We were on our way to another hotel a few blocks away. She tried to call for a new taxi for us, but none was available until the next morning. She tried to find us a room, but they were booked. So, she cheerfully said, "No problem – I will drive you there myself." As she drove us the few blocks, we asked a few questions. She had just started at the Marriott about two weeks ago. She had learned quickly that Marriott was all about service and doing

11

The best companies bring their brand to life collectively.

the right things for customers. But, we weren't even customers that night, we reminded her. No problem, she said. We very well could be next week, and she was happy to help us.

The best companies bring their brand to life collectively. As the playmaker, marketing sets the strategy and educates the company. But individuals and departments do most of the work. Thinking back to FedEx, if you want to build a strong, consistently powerful global brand, don't you have a better chance of achieving success if you have all 280,000 employees focused on the same thing?

When everyone owns the brand and everyone lives the brand, the brand takes on a life of its own. Every touch point then tells your consumers why your brand should be their choice. Marketing doesn't own the brand – the entire company does.

TRUTH

4

Making more by doing less

The most fundamental goal of branding is to generate profits for the brand holder. Every decision should be evaluated through the lens of profitability. Brand development is not about brand awareness, not about sales volume or market share and not about how cool your brand is. Brand development is about the long-term profitability of your brand.

Ironically, your business can be more profitable by doing less – focusing on a few things and doing those few things very well. But you must avoid the temptation to grow for the sake of growth; you must put aside personal or corporate ego that buys into the "bigger is better" and "size matters" myths.

> Your business can be more profitable by doing less – focusing on a few things and doing those few things very well.

US burger chain Hardee's struggled for a number of years. Adrift in the highly competitive fast food market, there was little that made Hardee's special. With competitors such as McDonald's, Wendy's and Burger King (as well as nonburger options such as Subway), Hardee's was in a weak position – and losing money.

Under the leadership of a new CEO, Hardee's simplified its menu, actually reducing the variety of offerings. Hardee's built its brand around the Thickburger hamburger – a differentiated product – and focused on people interested in "burger decadence". Hardee's closed weak-performing stores. The result of this transformation was lower total sales, fewer stores and *increased* profitability. Hardee's made more by doing less.

Monsanto is another company currently enjoying a bounty of success, but it hasn't always been that way. Before its current CEO, the company had a year of almost two billion dollars of losses and a stock price languishing in the single digits. Monsanto had been a conglomerate with operations covering a variety of areas in the chemical, pharmaceutical and agricultural industries.

In 2002, Monsanto was spun off as its own independent company after a couple of mergers and acquisitions. Now focused solely on agriculture, Monsanto passionately devotes its business towards improving crop-growing productivity and efficiency. Monsanto employs 3,000 research scientists focused on biotechnology research to ensure that the company maintains its strong position. Monsanto has focused its seed technologies on primarily four crops: corn, oilseeds (soya beans and oilseed rape), cotton and vegetables. With a more narrow focus on seed production, Monsanto is a smaller company than before – but a far more profitable one. Monsanto is making more by doing less.

Companies are finding that the power of their brands comes not from the wide range of markets they serve, but from doing a few things well. McDonald's sold the Boston Market and Chipotle restaurant chains in the US to focus attention on improving its own outlets. There's an old proverb that "A man who chases two rabbits catches neither."

It takes management discipline to stay focused on the core business. But such focus can create organisational power – everyone aligned around just a few things. Folk wisdom tells us not to put all our eggs in one basket. But, with all our eggs in one basket, we watch that basket carefully! When a company's future is tied to just a couple of brands, those brands are managed carefully.

> Companies are finding that the power of their brands comes not from the wide range of markets they serve, but from doing a few things well.

Turning around businesses such as Hardee's and Monsanto certainly required more than just brand focus. Hardee's new CEO spent time in the restaurants to simplify operations and understand better the customer experience. The restaurants were significantly overhauled to create a nostalgic feel. Developing a differentiated offering – the Thickburger brand – contributed to its turnaround. Monsanto's CEO shifted the culture to be more intense and results-oriented. Additionally, Monsanto has developed key technological collaborations including with one of its major competitors.

There are many contributing factors to a company's success. But the focus should always be on profitability – and you may find that you can make more by doing less.

TRUTH

5

Does your brand keep its promise?

People often ask, "What is a brand?" Consider a brand as a promise that you make to your consumers. That promise has two parts to it: what you say you are promising and what you actually deliver. As a brand, you must be true to your word.

As with any promise, once you make it, you have to keep it. Brand managers make promises through the perceptions they create, from the images they develop, the advertising they create, the promotions they offer, the packaging they use and the pricing they establish. Every one of these vehicles, among others, is communicating that brand promise.

Your performance speaks to how your product works and the service levels you provide. Your performance and perceptions must be in sync or you are breaking your promise; you are devaluing your brand.

The FedEx brand promises overnight delivery. You can send your package with confidence that it will arrive at the right spot, the next day. FedEx uses its advertising, its trucks and its entire culture to develop and reinforce this perception. But what happens when you don't receive your package on time? It didn't perform. You distrust its service; it did not keep its promise to you. FedEx is an outstanding brand because it routinely keeps its promise. Its performance is consistent with the perceptions it creates.

> Your performance and perceptions must be in sync or you are breaking your promise; you are devaluing your brand.

Brand managers are routinely charged with developing ideas to drive their brand's business. This pressure is more intense when there is a lack of product performance. When there are no new products in a pipeline, the marketing charge becomes "just create something fun and exciting". However, nothing can destroy a brand more quickly than creating expectations, interest and promises about something that doesn't exist. Consumers will be committed and loyal to a brand until that trust is broken. When the trust is broken, it may take years before the brand can re-establish itself.

One of the most famous examples of this occurred with Coca-Cola. Coke decided in the late '80s to introduce a new formulation but still call it Coke. Within weeks, the consumers revolted – so, Coke brought back its original formulation and called the new formula New Coke. At the very core, Coke had changed the performance of the brand but hadn't considered the effect that change would have on the promise of the brand that stood for so much in the consumer's mind.

Nothing can destroy a brand more quickly than creating expectations, interest and promises about something that doesn't exist.

More recently, a number of toy products, particularly those manufactured by Mattel, were found to have lead contamination. Although the contamination was from the manufacturing sites in China, the promise of the Mattel brand was damaged. Parents weren't sure that they could trust Mattel to provide safe toys for their children. Of course, Mattel was not the only manufacturer affected by this manufacturing concern. However, as a leader in toys, it bore the brunt of this situation. Toy retailers, also with a brand promise of providing safe toys, took Mattel to task as well. The promise of safety had been broken, and regardless of the cause, it was a reflection on the Mattel brand.

A similar situation occurred with tainted pet food. Again, the products were imported from China. However, it is the brand's name that is at risk when there is a product problem. In this case, many leading brands from Nestlé to Iams were impacted as their promises were broken and animals were getting sick. Once again, the promise of safety was broken for the consumer.

The cost of correcting the broken promise of a brand can be staggering. Marketing needs to be extremely clear on what the brand is truly delivering. As difficult as it is to do, standing up for a brand and ensuring that the messages of the brand don't get ahead of the performance that can actually be delivered is a critical function of brand management.

Before you build your brand, look at the gaps between your perceptions and performance. Be honest. Just because you want your brand to perform a certain way does not mean that it does. Evaluate what you should change. Is your brand performance too low? Are you creating lofty perceptions? Line them up.

Now go and build your brand by truly delivering against the promise you make.

TRUTH

6

Price is the communication of the value of your brand

Your brand possesses an assortment of attributes and meanings. Your brand connects with your consumer in both rational and emotional ways. Your brand also provides financial value to the company. Your brand is the source of your company's profits. Your brand's attributes, meanings and rational and emotional connections are sold, via the marketplace, to your customer.

When a family goes to Disney World, they are buying the park, the exhibits, the rides, the food and the employees who ensure everything runs smoothly. They are buying entertainment. They are buying memories. They are buying an icon of childhood. They are buying being a good parent. All of this represents value to the customer – value worth paying for. Disney creates this total experience in part because it reflects who it is as a business, and in part because this experience is desired by a segment of the market. Disney is investing in a brand experience that people find desirable. The price of this Disney adventure should be commensurate with the value it has created.

Price is the cost of the bundle of attributes and meanings called "your brand". The price you charge reflects the value of your brand – whether you intend it to. The greater the perceived value, the greater the price your brand commands. The more you have distinguished yourself from your competitors, the less vulnerable your brand is to their pricing strategies.

When you price low to gain market share, you say to potential customers, "My brand is not worth much." When you discount your service to meet short-term sales goals, you declare, "My brand is usually priced too high." When you regularly offer coupons on your product to attract price-sensitive consumers, you fail to appreciate the value the brand represents for your loyal customer base.

> The price you charge reflects the value of your brand – whether you intend it to or not. The greater the perceived value, the greater the price your brand commands.

Price represents more than just money from a sale. Price is more than just cost plus 25% markup. Price represents the value of your brand's attributes, associations and meaning.

Often, companies feel competitive pressure to reduce the price of their brand (either directly by lowering selling price or indirectly by raising discounts). A mistaken emphasis on market share or sales volume (rather than profits) drives this pressure. A desire to expand the appeal of the brand also leads management to reduce the price of the brand. But these actions communicate directly the value of the brand – and will have long-term consequences.

Izod Lacoste drove itself to the brink of extinction through price reductions. Created as a moderately upmarket brand of clothing, General Mills bought the brand in the '80s. Intent on capitalising on the positive image of the brand and maximising sales, General Mills lowered the quality of the clothes, expanded distribution and reduced price. In the short run, this worked, as the brand became more accessible to a larger market and sales increased. However, this move planted the seed of the brand's demise. Izod's reduced exclusivity and lower quality made the brand less appealing to its traditional constituency. And, as the brand held less value to its more affluent market, it became less appealing to the masses – whose original attraction to the brand was as a status symbol. The lower the price, the less valuable the brand.

Reducing the price of your brand seems appealing in the short run – having potential for increased sales, and being more appealing to a larger market. But caution is in order. In the long run, as your price erodes, your brand erodes.

What is your brand known for? What key associations, emotional or rational, have you developed around your brand? Developing satisfying answers to those two

In the long run, as your price erodes, your brand erodes.

questions is the essence of strong brand management. In developing your brand meaning and attributes, focus on those things that your target consumer values so much that they are willing to pay for them. Starbucks has created a brand experience in the US that commands four dollars for a cup of speciailty mocha (venti, please).

One goal of marketing is to give consumers a reason (or reasons) other than price to choose your brand. Your brand's meaning is one of these reasons. Callaway's innovative over-sized drivers give some golfers a clear reason to prefer its brand (and pay a significant price premium).

Pricing decisions are not simple. There are a number of factors to be considered. Are your competitors moving up or down with prices? What is projected for your labour and materials costs? Do you have a sense of price elasticity (are consumers relatively sensitive or insensitive to price?) for your brand? Are there industry watchdogs influencing pricing? Are you achieving your profit objective? One important factor is the signal your price communicates regarding the value your brand provides. The better your brand connects with your customers, the more indispensable your brand becomes as part of their life. The more emotionally connected your customers become to your brand and the better your brand meets the needs your customers have, the more pricing flexibility you will have.

The better your brand connects with your customers, the more indispensable your brand becomes as part of their life.

TRUTH

7

Brand personality is the emotional connection with your brand

Marketing and branding strive to connect you with your target consumer. The consumer can have an awareness of your brand. This awareness is recognition of your brand but not necessarily an understanding of what your brand represents. A consumer can connect with your brand intellectually. Such a connection reflects knowledge of the brand's features and benefits – for example, people may have an understanding that Cif provides tough cleaning power. Finally, a consumer can connect with your brand emotionally – to have a visceral feeling of the richness of the brand.

The proliferation of brands has led to a proliferation of similar brands. Pennzoil, Valvoline and Castrol – a chemist could probably explain the difference, but to many people they are all just good engine oils. What about Charmin and Andrex? Aren't they both just toilet paper? Pour Coke and Pepsi into glasses and what do you have? Basically carbonated sugar water. Competing effectively requires differentiation.

Creating compelling physical differences between brands is difficult – and is made more difficult by the ease at which those physical differences can be replicated.

Competing effectively requires differentiation.

Antilock brakes were once a valuable and unique characteristic of expensive cars, but now it is unusual for any model not to have antilock brakes. Brand personality, though, can add a differentiating dimension to consumers' understanding of your brand – a dimension not so easily duplicated; a dimension that can serve as your brand's important point of distinction.

Energizer and Duracell have long been battling in the battery market. Their slogans are parity claims – Duracell's "nothing tops the coppertop" and Energizer's "nothing outlasts Energizer". American consumers, though, see distinct differences in each brand's personality. Duracell is viewed as serious, dependable and tough. Consumers perceive Energizer as fun, hip and cool. Each brand's personality will be attractive to a different type of consumer.

With brand personality, you create an image of the brand, as if that brand were a person. You instil the brand with characteristics,

Brand personality can add a differentiating dimension to consumers' understanding of your brand – a dimension not so easily duplicated; a dimension that can serve as your brand's important point of distinction.

carefully defined, that bring the brand to life. Be sure to stay focused on those characteristics that reflect actual personality traits. Examples are personality characteristics such as outgoing, wacky, caring, reflective, brash and competitive.

The MasterCard campaign has done a great job of infusing emotion into its brand. The ads, both print and television, portray a touching moment – and the prices of things that make up that moment. The ads close by declaring the moment itself to be "priceless". The campaign takes a brand that has historically played second fiddle to Visa and imbues it with a touching sense of warmth, intimacy and tenderness. MasterCard becomes a gentle and kind friend, not simply another way to process a transaction.

In developing a brand personality, build the personality around, at most, three characteristics – more than that, and the brand becomes muddled. Consider also that the brand's personality is not identical to your consumer's personality. Some marketers make the mistake of turning their target audience description into a brand personality statement. Just because the target customer is sophisticated, intelligent and refined doesn't mean that the brand's personality must be.

In the US there was a great series of ads for kiwi fruit. The ads compared kiwis to more familiar fruit. In the ads, the kiwi talks to another featured fruit. A grapefruit challenges the kiwi with the line, "You're kind of small for a spoon, aren't you, kiwi?" The kiwi retorts, "I taste big, sourpuss. Sweet without sugar." In an ad with a banana, the banana says, "I taste good, you taste good. I've got potassium, you've got potassium. So?" To which the kiwi replies, "So, monkey see, monkey do." This great campaign gave factual information about kiwi fruit but also created a personality around kiwi as quick-witted, brash and saucy. That doesn't mean that the target consumer's personality was quick-witted, brash and saucy, however. Your brand's personality should be appealing to your target but not the same as your target.

The soft drinks market is highly competitive, with brands such as Coca-Cola, Pepsi-Cola, Tango and Dr Pepper battling for consumer affection. Certainly there are taste differences among these brands. But these brands work to create emotional connections through personality differences. Coke is more traditional, mainstream. Pepsi has long nurtured a more youthful brand image, striving to connect with contemporary young people. Tango has expanded sales with street-wise humour in the UK. Dr Pepper has a history of casting itself as independent, off-beat and eclectic. Each brand creates a personality that some segment of the market will respond to. Each brand's focus is more on its unique personality, not physical differences.

Yes, facts and knowledge about your brand are important. Facts and knowledge create an intellectual connection. Creating an interesting personality around your brand helps as well – it helps create an *emotional* connection with your consumer.

8

Does your sales force know
the difference between a
product and a brand?

Many salespeople sell products – items consisting of features and benefits.

"This car has 0.71 cubic metres of luggage space."

"We promise delivery within 48 hours."

"Our parts are machined to the highest tolerances in the industry."

This is all product talk; all statements about attributes. Good salespeople are trained not to focus solely on attributes but to turn the attribute into a benefit:

- "0.71 cubic metres of luggage space" becomes convenience for the busy family and family trips are made easy and comfortable.

- "Delivery within 48 hours" translates into quick possession.

- "Delivery within 48 hours" may for a business mean lower inventory requirements and reduced carrying costs.

- "Machined to the highest tolerances" means fewer headaches on the production line.

Great salespeople, though, are trained to focus on the brand and the fuller meaning that the brand brings. Not that storage space (and comfortable trips), fast delivery (and quick possession) and well-crafted parts (with fewer worries) aren't something that can be even more compelling to consumers – but emotion and imagery are.

A brand is more than features and benefits. A brand also represents a complex set of imagery. This imagery is often as motivating and relevant as the objective features and benefits of the product.

The Land Rover provides great carrying capacity...but the brand represents adventure. This adventure theme is reflected in the name. Ads for Land Rover focus less on specific attributes and more on the spirit of a brand that can transport you to anywhere in the world, and, as depicted in one TV ad, to the end of the Earth. Land Rover salespeople need to be

Great salespeople are trained to focus on the brand and the fuller meaning that the brand brings.

TRUTH

8

DOES YOUR SALES FORCE KNOW THE DIFFERENCE BETWEEN A PRODUCT AND A BRAND?

as well versed in the meaning of the brand as they are in product attributes, such as towing capacity and clearance height.

FedEx provides overnight delivery...but the brand delivers confidence. Budweiser refreshes on a hot afternoon...but the brand reflects a touch of American heritage and tradition.

Salespeople who have part of their pay tied to sales of their product or service will sometimes be too quick to call for price concessions or special discounting programmes to meet end-of-quarter sales quotas. Although understandable, this enthusiasm for price reductions can weaken the brand, which, ideally, should be competing effectively on some characteristics other than price.

Your sales force needs to understand not just the features and benefits of the product (or service) they are selling, but also the emotions and imagery of the brand. They need to understand how the brand makes an emotional connection with the end user – and that this emotional connection has value. They need to see meanings that the customer has wrapped around the brand. They need to recognise that while price is important, it should not be the primary point of emphasis in selling the brand.

The brand team, as the steward of the brand's meaning, works hard to discover and manage consumer perceptions. The brand team must also train the sales force in the meaning of the brand. The brand team should ensure that the sales force understands the brand's positioning (primary association) and equities (supporting associations). The sales force should see how the brand's marketing mix – advertising, public relations, website, product brochures and special promotions – all work in harmony to create a consistent, cohesive and clear brand image.

TRUTH

9

Beware of the discounting minefield

On sale. Clearance sale. Holiday sale. 25% off. 50% off. It never ends. Roy Williams in *Wizard of Ads* describes constant promotion as the cocaine of advertising. That's a good analogy because discounts make us feel good in the short run (as marketing teams see sales gains) but risk killing the brand in the long run (by cheapening the brand's image and shrinking profit margins). As consumers become acclimatised to this activity, it takes larger "doses" to keep generating interest and sales gains.

The problem with discounting is that you can never go low enough. There will always be a competitor willing to be cheaper than you. And that simple point is the crux of the discounting dilemma. Although an organisation may agonise over a few per centage point shifts in a discount – should the sale be at 20 per cent or 25 per cent off – there are other competitors who will be willing to discount deeper to stimulate revenue and market share.

Discounting is a minefield, and one in which you will most certainly lose. Even if you are brave enough to offer the lowest prices and ultimately win the weekly volume award, you have eroded your brand in the process, losing a more precious element along the way: your brand's equity.

US supermarket Kmart attempted to revitalise itself. Enthusiastic CEO Charles Conaway brought in a slew of fancy executives from places like Wal-Mart, Coca-Cola and Sears. The strategy for saving the brand? Compete head-on with Wal-Mart through extensive discounting. Really, that was it. Price reductions combined with extensive consumer promotions communicated through a steady stream of direct mail. Ultimately, this strategy led to bankruptcy, the departure of Mr Conaway, and finally a merger with one of Kmart's competitors.

Competing on price is the weakest of positions. First, marketing should provide consumers with a reason, other than price, to do business with you. Target understands this. Although competing in the domain of discounters, Target has created itself as a hip discounter in the US through creative merchandise selections and interesting advertising. Second, Wal-Mart's success with its low-price focus is due in large part to brutally efficient operations – an efficiency that Kmart was unable to match. Third, competing directly with a dominant market leader is rarely the path to success. Brands are built not through imitation but through differentiation. What logic could lead anyone to believe that Kmart could out-Wal-Mart Wal-Mart?

Competing on price is the weakest of positions. Marketing should provide consumers with a reason, other than price, to do business with you.

The battery wars are interesting to watch from a pricing perspective. Duracell has a slight US market share lead over Energizer. Rayovac is a distant third in market share. Rayovac is always the cheapest at point of sale of the national brands. Duracell is typically the market leader and the price leader at point of sale, striving to keep a 5-cent to 10-cent price advantage over Energizer. But, don't be confused – in the battery world, a price advantage for Duracell is being priced a few cents *above* Energizer. Why? Because Duracell understands that the price leader is often seen as the market leader, the quality and performance leader. All are brand attributes that relate back to a 5-cent to 10-cent price differential over their competitor, Energizer.

You can just see the Energizer sales associate proudly telling the head of marketing that he had secured a 5-cent discount versus Duracell. The sales team cheers because of the short-term volume potential. The marketing executive groans because once again, Duracell is positioned as a leader simply by premium pricing at point of sale.

Too many times, marketers convince themselves that the discount is just this one time. A temporary price reduction (TPR) is taken at a grocery store. A coupon of significant value is dropped across the county. A special buy one get one free (BOGOF) programme is provided for a mass merchandiser. The next thing you know, the consumer has become trained to wait for discounts. Your brand is now known for being sold below its recommended retail price and a little brand erosion has begun.

Discounting is a minefield because you never quite know when a discounting move will blow up on you. At what point has the consumer become so used to a promotional price that they refuse to purchase your product when it is not on sale? At what point is your competitor so desperate that it will drop prices significantly to capture your volume? If you do not have strong brand equity, if it has been declining because of price discounts, can your brand sustain such a pricing blow?

There is no denying that it is a fine line to walk – the balance between short-term gains from discounts and the damage to long-term brand building. But, be careful about over-promotion and extensive discounting. Walking into that minefield led Kmart to bankruptcy court.

TRUTH

10

Packaging protects your product; great packaging protects your brand

Packaging is an important component in the marketing of a brand. Certainly, it provides important functional benefits to the product. It keeps the product safe, protects it, provides a means for displaying it and is a communication vehicle. But, stop there, and packaging is not providing its potential value. Great packaging contributes to the success of the brand.

There was a poster ad that said: "Quick, Name a Soft Drink." On it was the picture of a Coca-Cola bottle. What was missing was the name Coca-Cola. This is the power of great packaging. Coca-Cola does not even need to place its actual brand name on the bottle; everyone recognises the brand by its packaging. Consider Pringles. Pringles differentiated itself from the myriad of crisp brands through the uniform shape of each crisp in a distinctive package cylinder in a category where every other brand comes in a bag. Not only does the package visually distinguish Pringles from its competitors, but, importantly, it also reinforces the brand's unique distinction of uniform shape. The strong connection between the brand name, the packaging and a key product attribute remains one of the great lessons in the power of packaging to drive a brand.

The heartburn remedy Nexium is known in the US as "the purple pill". Encased in a purple gel cap, Nexium has established the colour of the package as a powerful equity. Similarly, Viagra has become known as the little blue pill. Again, both the colour (blue) and shape (diamond) have become important packaging equities for this pharmaceutical brand.

Tiffany operates in a competitive luxury jewellery market. And, its trademark blue box provides a recognisable point of distinction sure to bring a smile to the gift recipient.

Packaging engages with the customer – and can increase or decrease the customer's satisfaction with the product experience. Americans love Oreo cookies but become maddeningly frustrated with the packaging. They try to open the package carefully – but the inevitable long tear down the plastic hampers keeping them fresh. There is no good way to reseal the package. People fold over the plastic and stack soup cans on top. Or wrap up the whole package in clingfilm...and then have to fiddle with the film every time they return for a few cookies. They have finally said "forget it". The package has failed the brand.

Simple packaging ideas enhance the customer's experience, such as grated cheese that comes in an easy-to-open, resealable bag. Tide laundry detergent includes a measuring scoop inside the box. There was a little-known US brand called Glacier beer. The bottom of the bottle had a cutout in the shape of a twist-off bottle opener – you could simply use the bottom of one bottle to open the other. The issue of opening the last one aside, what a delightful package idea for enhancing the customer's ease of use! Your package is an intimate connection with your customer. Make it a connection that facilitates, not frustrates, the use of your brand.

Packaging can also serve to enhance and reinforce brand image. A US company called Pinnacle Natural Brilliance makes Souveran, an expensive car wax. Souveran consumers are drawn to the quality of the actual wax – a rich, buttery, 100% carnuba. Pinnacle Natural Brilliance has invested in packaging that reinforces Souveran's high-end image. The box for Souveran is a rich black with labels in primarily red and gold. Opening the box reveals a nice "thank you" note from the

> Your package is an intimate connection with your customer. Make it a connection that facilitates, not frustrates, the use of your brand.

company. A gold pouch inside the box contains the jar of wax. The jar is in the same black, red and gold colours. A wax applicator (gold) and a microfibre towel (royal blue with a gold wrapper) are also included for removing the wax. Much thought has gone into creating a package that reinforces the brand's image (and high price!).

Tea Embassy, a speciality tea house in the US, sells a variety of quality loose teas. The family who runs the business is extremely knowledgeable about tea. Purchased tea is scooped into resealable protective pouches. Then a label is affixed to the pouch. The label indicates, of course, the type of tea. Importantly, though, the label also specifies exact directions for getting the maximum drinking enjoyment. ("Steep one tablespoon per cup for two minutes in below boiling water about 180 degrees F.") Tea Embassy also uses the label to provide information about the tea. Natela's Gold says, "Lifelong Georgian tea artisan, Natela, prepared this special batch of black tea near the Black Sea." The simple tea package reinforces Tea Embassy's expertise.

Yes, your packaging has to protect your product. Yes, it has to communicate information. Yes, your package needs to provide a means for displaying your product. But, most importantly, your package must reinforce your brand's distinction. Does your package have a unique shape (like Coca-Cola) or a unique colour (like Tiffany)? Does your package communicate your brand's differentiation (like Pringles)? Does your package contribute to the image of your brand (like Souveran or Tea Embassy)? The package is the last opportunity to communicate the brand before it is purchased. Is your packaging simply doing its job, or is it great?

TRUTH

11

Brand management is association management

Building, developing and maintaining a strong brand requires management of a brand's associations. It is these associations, reinforced consistently over time, that give a brand its meaning. What does the brand "Nike" mean? Maybe athletics, determination, running and performance? What about the brand "iPod"? Perhaps music to go, hip and easy to use? Do these meanings come through by accident? Of course not. Brands with solid, clear meanings are carefully designed and nurtured.

Effectively managing your brand's associations requires an understanding of the basic structure of human memory, for it is in memory (the mind) that a brand lives. Memory is simply a collection of nodes and links between those nodes. For example, the node in memory labelled "Paris" might have associative links to the nodes "romance", "Metro" and "riots".

Brands with solid, clear meanings are carefully designed and nurtured.

Brands, of course, are also nodes linked with other nodes. For example, the brand "UPS" might be linked to "brown", "package delivery", "reliable" and "courteous drivers". Because brands exist in memory, not every person is going to have the same set of associations for a given brand. Powerful brands, though, strive to be reasonably consistent as to the set of associations around the brand and strive to have the same associations linked to the brand from person to person.

These associations around a brand vary in the strength of the link with the brand. The brand Starbucks might have a strong link to "green" or "relaxing ambiance" and a weaker link to "music". The strength of the link reflects the likelihood of that association coming to mind when people think of the brand. Brands, therefore, want strong links with associations that matter.

Developing these strong links to relevant and differentiating associations is a key task of brand management. And there are fundamental principles that guide the formation and strengthening of these links.

One of the most basic principles for developing strong associations is repetition. Repetition reinforces the link between the brand and the association. DeBeers' use of "Diamonds are Forever" year after year builds a strong association between diamonds and "timelessness". Wheaties' repetitive use of "Breakfast of Champions" strengthens the association between the breakfast cereal and winners.

One of the most basic principles for developing strong associations is repetition.

Consistency, related to repetition, is another important principle that facilitates strengthening the link between a brand and an association. Be consistent over time, as in the DeBeers and Wheaties examples, but also be consistent across communication modes. Michelin has used the Michelin Man since 1898 (consistency over time) and also uses the Michelin Man in much of its advertising, its website and in tyre dealerships (consistency across marketing tools). This consistency helps strengthen the relationship between the brand Michelin and this symbol of trustworthiness.

Brand managers at times want to add a new association to a brand. Adding associations to a brand can be a challenge. The more associations a brand already has, the more difficult it is to add a new association. Think of associations as competing for a place connected to the brand. If a brand has a number of strong associations in place, it is difficult for the newcomer to find a good spot to attach itself to the brand. This is one reason why it is difficult to change perceptions of a long-standing, well-known brand.

A brand's meaning is much more elastic early in the brand's life, before many associations have taken hold strongly. Also, some brands have been around for a long time but have never developed strong, clear associations in the minds of consumers. These brands also have some flexibility in adding new associations.

It is easier to add an association when it is consistent with the existing associations for the brand. For example, if a brand has the associations "youthful", "contemporary" and "fast", it is much easier to add the association "fun" than if the brand's associations were "serious", "dependable" and "competitive". "Fun" is simply more consistent with the first set of associations than the second set.

When designing the set of associations for your brand, start with an understanding of the current associations your customers have for the brand. Your best strategy may be to reinforce those. Also, associations can be added more easily to your brand if they are consistent with your brand's current associations. Don't overreach with the number of associations you want to develop around your brand. Choose perhaps three or four powerful ones. Brands, particularly those that have been around for some time, can have a number of associations in their orbit; but you want to choose the three or four stars – the associations that are most relevant and distinguishing – to build your brand around. You should focus your communication activities around those three or four associations, which will be your brand drivers. Look for ways to integrate those associations across your communication vehicles – advertising, website, sales force, public relations, package and point-of-sale materials. Stick with those associations over time. Brand management is association management.

TRUTH

12

The retail experience is the brand experience

Even with all the money spent in managing the communications around a brand, so much of a consumer's sense of a brand comes through the brand experience. This is particularly true in a retail environment where ensuring brand consistency can be more challenging than with the manufacturing of products.

The Apple Store is a great example of a retail experience that is consistent with and enhances the brand. With a clean, light layout, the computers are spaced for easy use by potential customers. The store colour scheme is integrated with the colours of the computers. The store atmosphere has a clean, minimalist feel. Employees are friendly, knowledgeable and accessible. The entire sense of the store reinforces the brand's image of a friendly, easy-to-use and stylish computer. Small decisions, such as naming the help desk something creative like "Genius Bar", reinforces Apple's brand image.

Although the size of the Apple Stores varies – for example, the main Chicago one is on two stories, whereas the St Louis stores are smaller and in shopping centres – each location creates a similar brand feel.

Successful brands strive to maintain a consistency in presentation. Retail brands, with operations sometimes flung worldwide, require extra vigilance. Porsche, with showrooms across the globe, has been moving towards dealerships that carry only its brand (as opposed to dealerships that feature a number of marques). Porsche has created a uniform look for dealerships in countries as diverse as the US, Mexico, Great Britain, Singapore and its home country of Germany. The design specifications were set by Porsche and create an exclusive and distinctive look. Steel and aluminium exterior, metal used in the interior and black walls and floors create a consistent visual feel designed to highlight its cars and reinforce a contemporary, technologically advanced image.

Since 2000, Porsche has opened more than 500 of these "Porsche Centres" around the world. An international network of architects, known as "brand guardians", help coordinate the design and development of the individual dealerships – each of which requires an average investment of €2.1 million. Although the individual dealerships vary with respect to size and physical configuration, they all are adapted to the brand look first created in Stuttgart. Although

Porsche sells its cars in markets that vary widely with respect to economic, social and political influences, Porsche recognises the value in a unified global look.

Similarly, BMW has worked with its motorcycle dealers to upgrade and standardise its retail look and feel. Motorcycle dealerships can have a casual, gritty flavour. BMW wants dealerships that have a more contemporary, upmarket sense that reflects more closely its desire for the brand.

Sometimes the retail experience can run counter to the general direction of a brand. Wolfgang Puck is a culinary luminary in the US. His restaurants are widely acclaimed, and his brand has an upmarket feel to it. Chicago's O'Hare airport had a retail kiosk called Wolfgang Puck Express. Selling soft drinks, sweets and odds and ends, this retail venture, while no doubt making a profit from a captive audience, risks cheapening the Wolfgang Puck image. Such a disconnect between an elite culinary brand and a mini-mart probably does little to add to the exclusive image Wolfgang Puck has created with his restaurants.

Inventory assortment is part of the brand experience and should be managed to reinforce the brand's key focus. The selections that customers encounter in the shop create an impression of what that retail brand represents. Keep your inventory consistent with your brand.

A Passport Luggage shop in the US will have the expected displays of luggage. Also sold there are ancillary items such as briefcases, backpacks and Swiss Army knives – all items, although not technically luggage, that are related to travel. The name "Passport Luggage" creates an image around travel and adventure. The name creates expectations about the brand experience and the kinds of items to be found there.

Inventory assortment is part of the brand experience and should be managed to reinforce the brand's key focus.

One shop also had a nice display cabinet of Waterford Crystal. Hmmm...now that's interesting! Probably somewhere along the line, someone found some research that people who travel are more likely than average to buy fine crystal. So, being logical business people, it only made sense that Passport Luggage would add Waterford to the store inventory.

The problem with this logic is that it seems highly unlikely that someone shopping for luggage would make an impulse purchase of expensive crystal. And it seems equally unlikely that when actively in the market for fine crystal, someone would think to go to a luggage store. Much later, sensibility prevailed and the display was removed. Displaying and selling Waterford Crystal simply wasn't part of the brand design for Passport Luggage.

Creating a powerful retail experience begins with a commitment to consistency. It begins with an understanding of what the brand is intended to mean. It begins with an appreciation for how the brand meaning should shape the retail experience. It begins with the realisation that for retail brands, the retail experience is very much the brand experience.

Creating a powerful retail experience begins with a commitment to consistency.

TRUTH

13

Corporate ego: danger ahead

Confidence is great. Confidence supplies the fortitude to forge ahead in a bold way. Overconfidence and hubris, though, can result in many bad branding and marketing decisions.

Wal-Mart has seen great success – providing basic goods to millions of Americans at affordable prices. Wal-Mart no doubt employs many bright and educated people charged with making sound decisions to move its business ahead. These bright and educated managers are not, however, immune to judgement clouded by overconfidence. With intent to expand its customer base, Wal-Mart began to move into more expensive,

Overconfidence and hubris can result in many bad branding and marketing decisions.

fashionable clothing. This move failed – that is not how people knew Wal-Mart. Even more affluent customers who shop at Wal-Mart for deals on household basics like laundry detergent aren't going to be so interested in purchasing clothes there. Wal-Mart recently abandoned DVD rentals and downloads. Apparently, competing with Netflix wasn't such a good idea. Wal-Mart's music download business will almost certainly never approach the success of Apple's iTunes. To applause from investors, Wal-Mart is reorientating itself to its fundamental mission of selling basic goods at attractive prices – a little bit of a corporate ego reality check.

Talbots has made a good name for itself with clothing designed for the professional American woman – and the brand has come to mean just that. Talbots men and children stores (first opened in 2006 and 1993, respectively) have been a failure and are now being closed down. That a brand associated with women would be successful in attracting men could only be attributed to a case of overblown corporate ego.

Snapple, a US beverage company, was formed by three health food store owners in 1972. Snapple's iced teas (first introduced in 1987) began to build success for its business, and Snapple's advertising had a home-spun, down-to-earth feel to it, reflected by Wendy the Snapple lady. Seeing the growing success of Snapple, and no doubt certain it could do a much better job managing the brand, Quaker

Oats bought Snapple for $1.7 billion in 1994. Unfortunately for Quaker shareholders, the Snapple lady was probably a better brand manager than the high-powered Quaker marketing managers. Three years later, Quaker abandoned ship and sold off Snapple at a $1.3 billion loss.

US bleach maker Clorox recently purchased Burt's Bees for close to a billion dollars. With a reputation of eco-friendliness, Burt's Bees' products sell at a nice premium against similar mass-marketed brands. Clorox will need to preserve the integrity of the Burt's Bees brand to ensure that its investment was a wise one for its shareholders. Clorox will need to do a better job than Quaker Oats did with Snapple in not losing the special noncorporate aura that has led to Burt's Bees' success.

The brain child of then-chairman Ferdinand Piech, the $100,000 VW Phaeton was a colossal failure. VW employs many bright, sharp people. Clearly, some of those bright people could see the folly of trying to sell a six-figure Volkswagen. Who, though, is going to walk into the chairman's office and challenge him on his own pet project? Only someone otherwise close to retirement!

Ford chalked up almost *$5 billion* in losses over a recent four years under the misguided belief that it could successfully manage a set of European luxury brands. It has now sold off Aston Martin Jaguar and Land Rover. Ford has a proud history of designing and building cars for the middle class – and it has plenty of challenges just staying competitive in that market! Perhaps the luxury car business was biting off a bit more than it could chew.

Another US carmaker, Dodge, has signed licensing agreements that have included high-end Dolce & Gabbana t-shirts, garage floor surfaces, bicycles and dog bowls! With sales flagging and no-nonsense private equity firm Cerberus having taken over, Dodge management would be better served by figuring out how to sell more cars and trucks and be less concerned about how many dog bowls its logo appears on.

Nike sold off the Starter footwear and clothing brand it purchased after three years. A successful brand in its own right, Nike surely was confident it would find success with this lower-end brand. Ultimately, however, Nike acknowledged that its business would be better served by focusing on selling higher-priced shoes.

Payless is a low-end US shoe chain that specialises in...well, the name says it all. In response to slowing sales, Payless has begun to carry more stylish, trendier, higher-priced shoes, hoping to attract a younger, hipper consumer. But Payless risks alienating its current customer base. And, at the same time, it may fail to attract these new customers, who have plenty of other places to shop for more stylish shoes. Zales failed with this exact same strategy, fired its CEO, and reversed course to its original focus on affordable jewellery.

As if the fashion business weren't competitive enough, Armani announced that it is partnering with electronics producer Samsung to develop a line of high-end electronics. Time will certainly tell, but a luxury fashion brand not known for electronics combining with an electronics manufacturer not known for prestige goods sounds like the worst of both worlds driven by inflated corporate ego.

Success in one area does not automatically result in success in another area. That Wal-Mart management has been successful serving one part of the market does not mean that management can successfully take the Wal-Mart name into a different market. That Ford has mastery of selling cars to middle-class America does not mean it has a special capability to manage higher-end luxury brands. An overly inflated corporate ego can cause managers to overestimate their competencies and fail to see the limitations of their brands. Be humble, be honest, be true.

> **Success in one area does not automatically result in success in another.**

TRUTH

14

Brand metrics: best measure of success?

Brand metrics – measures of the effectiveness of marketing activity – have become all the rage of late. And for some good reasons. First, technological advances have facilitated gathering information. The prevalence of scanner data collected at large retailers, "people meters" that provide increased accuracy in tracking media usage, and the growth of measurement-friendly web commerce have all increased the amount of data available to marketing managers. Second, corporate boards are increasingly demanding accountability for marketing spending. Companies that have elevated the importance of marketing through the relatively new title "Chief Marketing Officer" are also elevating expectations of quantifiable performance. It is just smart business to ask: "What are we getting for our investment?"

Fundamentally, brand metrics are designed to measure and assess marketing activity. Brand metrics can be used (and misused) in a variety of ways. Because marketing and brand-building activity are designed to enhance profitability, the most relevant metric is return on investment (ROI). The idea is simple: for any marketing action, determine what sales were the direct result of the marketing action, determine the profit on those sales, subtract the cost of the marketing action and voilà – you are left with the incremental profit directly attributable to that marketing action.

Measuring the impact of marketing activity this way can work in certain instances when there is a close link between the marketing activity and sales. Consider a brand that runs long-format information-filled adverts. Air time is purchased. The "infomercial" runs with a unique response number keyed to that particular airing. Calls come in, units are sold, costs are easily attributed to that particular commercial and profit is tallied.

But what about the following example? A business-to-business company reserves stand space at a major trade show where a number of potential customers will be attending. The company dutifully totals up expenditures – travel and lodging, space rental, costs for a nice display, product brochures and salary for the company representatives working the stand. At the show, contacts are made and leads generated. After the show, salespeople make follow-up calls and sales orders come in. Two months later, an assessment is made of the effectiveness of attending the trade show. But wait...what about orders that came in within two months of the show but would have been placed anyway? What about a contact made that resulted in no order? And what if, a year later, when looking for a new supplier,

Accurately assessing the effect of much marketing activity can be very difficult.

that contact remembers the company they met at the trade show and requests a meeting with one of the sales representatives?

Consider a more involved example. A large consumer brand receives a significant increase in support. Packaging is revised, a new ad campaign is created, media spending is increased and an innovative consumer promotion is implemented. Sophisticated time series analysis can provide some retrospective assessment of the overall effectiveness of this effort but will leave questions about the relative influence of each individual component unanswered. Was it worth redesigning the package? Did the new ads make a difference (or was it just the increased media spending)? Assessing these individual tactics is extremely difficult.

Here are several thoughts for developing brand metrics for your business: don't be a slave to metrics, measure what matters, and keep an appropriate sense of perspective.

Don't be a slave to metrics. There will be important marketing objectives that are either impossible to quantify and measure or simply cost prohibitive to do so. For many companies, quantifying metrics like brand awareness and brand attitude is simply too expensive. Small and medium-sized companies don't have the market research budget to support measuring a wide assortment of metrics, regardless of how important those metrics might be. For example, the impracticality of measuring the effect of business-to-business advertising in trade publications does not mean that such advertising should be eliminated. Such advertising may be playing an important, albeit difficult to measure, role in supporting your brand.

In addition to ROI, there are many popular brand metrics, including brand awareness, sales, market share, repeat rate, brand attitude,

Choose those metrics that you believe are true profit drivers for your brand.

share of requirements (per cent of a consumer's category purchases that go to your brand), satisfaction and so on. Choose those metrics that you believe are true profit drivers for your brand. It's said that what is measured is what is managed. If you focus on things such as brand awareness and market share, you will get lots of those things – regardless of whether brand awareness and market share are actually linked to profitability.

Keep a sense of perspective on your use of brand metrics. Some marketing actions, like discounting, can have a positive short-term effect on metrics such as sales, trialling and market share, but hurt the value of your brand in the long run. Some marketing activity that is vitally important to the success of your business may have benefits that unfold over a particularly long horizon. Certainly John Deere expects its dealer activity to have some positive effect on sales of tractors and equipment to farmers. But John Deere works to build relationships with farmers that span generations. It's a little harder to directly measure the results of that!

Accountability expectations aren't going away. But brand metrics are not substitutes for good reason and judgement. Kept in perspective, brand metrics can provide some helpful guidance in assessing the impact of your marketing activity.

15

Customer complaints
are a treasure

Brand managers, on the whole, are terrified of customer complaints. Companies measure customer satisfaction, and declines in customer satisfaction are marks against a brand manager. Year-end reviews often include an assessment of brand likeability and, therefore, include complaints. However, a customer complaint is an opportunity to really understand what matters to the customer and to get a deeper understanding of the target audience.

Companies often promote the message that "the customer is always right". You have heard that before, but do the exchanges and the complaints actually translate into a better experience or product for the customer? Not always. You return a product to Tesco, for any reason, and you receive prompt, courteous service. The matter is taken care of, and the customer leaves happy. However, the manufacturer, or perhaps Tesco itself, is missing out on an enormous opportunity to understand what can be done to make the product better. Did the shirt not fit because the cut was wrong, which made it tight in the shoulders? Did the hair dryer not work out because the cord wasn't long enough? Did the household cleaner come back because the smell was too pungent? There is so much more depth to a complaint that is often missed.

> A customer complaint is an opportunity to really understand what matters to the customer and to get a deeper understanding of the target audience.

Lands' End is a company that strongly embraces customer complaints as treasure. It learns from them. It tells you what it learned, it makes adjustments in its product and it tries again. If you purchase from there and need to return a product, you will find detailed questions about the return. What part didn't fit? What was wrong with the fit? These questions are not done to "trick" the customer so that the return is not accepted. They are done to understand how it can design its clothes better. In fact, Lands' End clearly lets every customer know that anything can be returned at any time – there is no risk. It wants happy customers and, importantly, better products for those customers.

There is so much more depth to a complaint that is often missed.

Lands' End takes its commitment a bit further. Look closely in its catalogues and you will see references to its learning. "We heard you," it will often write, "and so we have cut the leg a bit narrower" or "extended the length of the shirt". Lands' End understands that customer complaints are a treasure, and it uses them to enhance its offer. In the end, Lands' End becomes a brand you can trust.

For years, J.D. Power has measured the quality of companies in the US by using the quality of customer service as one of its critical measures. Recently, T-Mobile won in wireless for being responsive on the phone, in the stores, answering concerns and complaints quickly and effectively. What makes a J.D. Power award noteworthy is that consumers help to determine the criteria for success.

But, as a brand, you don't need J.D. Power to help you understand what matters to a customer. You need only to listen to their complaints. They will tell you very directly.

A pharmacy retailer had a number of private label products, provided by a third-party supplier. The retailer started to get a consistent complaint from one particular woman about its own brand skin lotion. The woman had a cat who liked to lick the woman's arms. The cat started to get sick, and the woman deduced that it was the lotion that she had recently bought that had been the cause of the problem. Go ahead and laugh. The pharmacy retailer certainly did. The solution seemed obvious to most who worked there – don't let the cat lick your arm. However, one astute marketer asked, why were they just now getting that complaint? Doing a little investigation, it was discovered that the formulation of the lotion had changed ever so slightly – enough to make the cat ill. That knowledge helped the retailer work with its supplier so that no more changes could be made to formulations, no matter how minor, without its knowledge and permission.

In this instance, a minor complaint led to a change in purchasing procedures for a company. One can only imagine what other "minor" formulation changes could have done over the years to people, or other cats. This was a complaint that ended up being a true treasure.

Behind most complaints is a bit of knowledge that can help to improve a product or service; a complaint can provide a deeper understanding of a customer's needs. Treasure those complaints – they will make your brand stronger.

TRUTH

16

Brand stewardship begins at home

You know that raising a child with values begins at home, or that education begins at home, but what about a brand? A brand's home is its organisation. To build a successful brand, you must start at home. How can you possibly expect your customers to understand or be loyal to your brand if your own people don't understand your brand or brands? If your own people are not loyal?

Brand stewardship must have the commitment of the senior executives. If the executives don't recognise the importance of building their brands, that message will not be understood by the organisation. If the executives don't stay true to the meaning of the brand, to its messaging in the market, why should the rest of the organisation? With clarity from the executive team comes clarity for the organisation about the strength and value of the brands.

It is so easy for executives to say that the brand is owned by marketing and to not take a strong stand in the stewardship of the brand. Yet, the importance of stewarding the brand by everyone is

Brand stewardship must have the commitment of the senior executives.

most directly understood when the executives take the lead in driving the brand. They set the example for the rest of the organisation.

Importantly, brand stewardship must occur deep within the "soul" of the organisation. Every employee, whether they directly interact with customers, must live the brand. The brand helps to shape the tone of the culture. As the culture is shaped, it then serves to reinforce and build the brand. So, the culture, the brand and the employees are all directly related when it comes to delivering a brand experience.

Too many times we hear that the brand is just marketing's responsibility. But, the truth of the matter is, marketing is not the only group that touches the external market. So, every function that touches the external market must live the brand. If members of an organisation cannot deliver the brand experience to each other, how can they possibly take it in an effective manner to the marketplace? Stewarding the brand not only must start at home, but it also must start by providing the very values the brand stands for to its own employees.

Marriott has made a name for itself in service. But service for Marriott isn't just what happens at the front desk. Service is how employees treat employees. It is embodied by J.W. Marriott, the founder, sitting down and listening to an employee's personal problem because of the deeply held belief that they must serve each other to effectively serve their guests. By living the concept of service at Marriott, it becomes natural, and not another "to do" item on their list for the day.

Every function that touches the external market must live the brand.

Donatos is a smaller US chain of pizza parlours that also provide delivery. Its brand tagline is "Respect the Pizza". But, let's be honest... pizza is pizza, right? Absolutely wrong – and Donatos understands that in spades.

Some friends ordered pizzas from Donatos. As brand enthusiasts, we knew the tagline "Respect the Pizza". However, the group was flabbergasted at what happened at delivery. The delivery man showed up carrying the pizzas. As he handed them over, he asked, "Do you have plates?" We responded that we had napkins, so we were good. "Sir," he said, "Respect the pizza," and handed over several sturdy paper plates. The concept and the experience of Donatos pizza had reached all the way to the delivery person, who was now effectively stewarding the brand.

This was a wonderful experience. Here was a delivery man, with no one watching over his shoulder, advocating "Respect the Pizza" and offering plates because he respected the pizza. Isn't that always the telling story? What do your children do when you are not watching? How is your brand communicated when marketing is not involved?

What is powerful about this experience with Donatos is the totality of the messaging. Every aspect of the experience reinforced the message of "Respect the Pizza". We "respected" that pizza just a little bit more. The stewardship of the brand throughout the organisation ensured that we clearly understood the brand.

Living your brand begins by understanding your brand, and then taking that understanding and applying it to every detail of the business. Brand stewardship begins at the top. If your executives do not believe in the brand, and are not committed to the brand, why should your employees? Why should your consumers? Consider what your brand means and apply it to everything: the memos you write, the people you greet and the vendors who call. Watch and see the brand come alive throughout the organisation; watch it develop a life of its own; and watch the consumers become completely loyal to the brand. Respect the pizza.

TRUTH

17

Market share doesn't matter

Is growth desirable? Is market share a worthy goal? Most managers would answer unambiguously "yes". Actually, it depends. Increasing profit margins and return on equity typically enhances shareholder value. Simply getting bigger does not. Over a recent five-year period, Nike added three billion dollars in sales, yet only forty million dollars of profits – that's top-line growth with little effect on profitability. The stock market does not reward simply chasing market share and sales volume unless such growth leads to greater return on equity, generating profits more efficiently.

A friend, an IT vice-president at a large company, was talking about his company's history of acquisitions. Over the years, his company had added a number of smaller companies to its business. He was amazed that even though the company was growing in size, the stock price remained relatively flat. His story, though, wasn't a surprise. Unless the company becomes more efficient at generating profits, simply getting bigger isn't going to increase shareholder value.

The misguided quest to get larger can lead to marketing decisions that reduce the sharpness of the brand. In the US Starbucks and Dunkin' Donuts are encroaching on each other's turf. Dunkin' Donuts is pushing fancy cappuccino and espresso. Starbucks is opening locations in gritty, blue-collar neighbourhoods. Each brand risks diluting its core meaning. Starbucks is an inviting gourmet coffee experience and its choice of locations is an element of creating the brand's meaning. Dunkin' Donuts provides good, basic coffee – it simply isn't a cappuccino and espresso kind of place.

With athletic shoe sales relatively flat, Nike's head of clothing wants to double such sales to $6 billion in five years. The key strategy is to move beyond sports wear, treading on territory well covered by brands such as Gap and Tommy Hilfiger by creating "must-have outfits". The general fashion industry is brutally

Unless the company becomes more efficient at generating profits, simply getting bigger isn't going to increase shareholder value.

competitive, and pursuing this endeavour dilutes Nike's association with athletics. To Nike, we say, "Good luck!"

The press reports regularly on the battle for the title of the world's biggest carmaker, and in early 2007, Japan's Toyota claimed it had overtaken US rival General Motors to take the top spot. However, particularly in the US, rebates are often used to generate sales at the expense of profits. Such thinking is not confined to the motor industry, as many companies use discounting and loading gimmicks to boost end-of-year sales figures. Investors and the market, though, care not for market share and sales volume. Investors care only about the stream of positive cash flow – profits.

Recently, Wal-Mart earnings disappointed Wall Street. The culprits? Decreased profit margins from discounting to attract more shoppers, as well as Wal-Mart's failed attempt to increase market share by selling goods to more affluent shoppers.

In addition to profit problems, growth can cause other concerns. Toyota has been extremely successful, rising to be the number-two car brand (based on market share) in the US (behind General Motors and closing fast). But growth can bring problems. Toyota's J.D. Power quality ratings have dropped. And questions were raised about the declining quality of some models by consumer groups, even though Toyota still dominated lists of recommended vehicles.

Building a strong brand means that consumers see sufficient value in your offering that they pay a price that allows you to make a reasonable profit for your shareholders. Porsche and BMW are two of the most profitable brands in the car industry. Both are low share brands, concerned more with maintaining price premium via a strong brand image than they are with sales volume. They understand well that their primary responsibility to shareholders is profitability. Although clearly they have to operate at a sales level that ensures manufacturing efficiencies, they understand the discipline of brand building for profits. They avoid the allure of chasing market share.

Why this belief in the primacy of market share? In part, this belief stems from the power of economies of scale – as sales (and therefore production) go up, average cost per unit goes down. True...but these economies of scale are typically achieved quickly and at relatively low shares. In part, this belief stems from a perceived positive relationship between market share and profitability. But typically, market share *doesn't cause* profitability. Management skill and luck affect *both* market share and profitability simultaneously.

Lack of a nuanced understanding of market share and profitability relationships fosters a belief that market share *per se* causes profitability. Armed with this belief, companies will engage in market share-building activities (such as extensive consumer promotion or price discounting) that actually reduce profitability.

Extensive discounting and free service offers designed to pump up market share and customer counts attract the least loyal customers, further deteriorating the health of the business.

Such activity does not fool rational investors, who understand that unprofitable customers and market share built on profit-draining rebates don't serve their interests well. Investors don't care about market share. Profit is the nobler objective.

The myth that larger is better has been debunked but still thrives with many business leaders. The quest to get bigger can hurt a brand's image – and, in the end, isn't what really enhances shareholder value.

TRUTH

18

Avoid the most common segmentation mistake

Segmentation is a cornerstone of sound marketing and brand building. Segmentation is the forming of groups (of consumers) based on some criteria or characteristics. The usefulness of segmentation ties directly to how these groups are formed. Formed appropriately, segments can be a powerful organising principle for brand development. Used inappropriately, segmentation can weaken your understanding of the market you compete in. The most common mistake is to segment based on demographics (age, income, education, marital status and so on). Brand managers will say things like "our segment is young, affluent men" or "we've divided the market into three categories – low income, moderate income and high income". Both cases illustrate segmentation by demographics. The first example is a bit more sophisticated, but it is segmentation by demographics nonetheless.

Segmentation by demographics fails to provide deep insight into the underlying dynamics that are affecting brand choices. If segmenting by demographics is not that useful, how should you think about segmentation? There are three particularly good ways to segment the market – by profit, by behaviour and by benefit.

Segmentation by profit recognises that different people have different (financial) value to a business. A person can be valuable because they buy lots of your product or service. For example, a woman buying paper towels for a family of five is likely to buy a lot of paper towels. A person may be valuable because he or she is relatively insensitive to price and doesn't demand or expect discounts. A person may be valuable because his or her loyalty will generate revenue over many years. Segmentation, then, forms groups of people based on profitability. You can create as many groups as is useful for your business. For example, some banks use internal colour codes "red", "yellow" and "green" to reflect the profit importance of customers. A high-profit "green" customer

> Segmentation by demographics fails to provide deep insight into the underlying dynamics that are affecting brand choices.

will (and should) receive preferential treatment. Implementing segmentation by profit requires detailed data on revenue and costs at the customer level – data not available in many instances.

With segmentation by behaviour, groups are formed based on some unique characteristic relevant to the business. A retailer such as Home Depot might group customers into several behavioural segments such as "do-it-yourself renovator" (someone who takes on major renovation projects) or "weekend DIY guy" (someone who makes minor home repairs on the weekend). These segments are formed by behaviour, not demographics.

Segmentation by benefit is the third recommended segmentation approach. People vary with respect to what is the primary driving factor that influences their choice of brand. Consider cars. Some people most heavily value safety. For some, reliability is most important. For others, performance is the primary motivator. Consider jeans. In choosing a brand, some people are more focused on prestige. Some people value comfort. For others, low price is the primary consideration. Each of these examples illustrates a benefit segment.

Only after you have formed segments do demographics come into play. People in the "safety" segment for cars might tend to be female, 25–45 years old, married, with a household size of three to six. The "weekend DIY guy" segment might be characterised as male, 35–50 years old, suburban, with a household income of £25–75,000. But notice that demographics are not used to form the segments, but rather to *describe* the segments after they have been formed.

> There are three particularly good ways to segment the market – by profit, by behaviour and by benefit.

Segmentation provides value in two ways – it improves both the effectiveness and the efficiency of your marketing efforts. By very clearly identifying a target group, you can gain deep insight into the motivations of that group – what advertising appeals will work, what types of promotion will be compelling and what product or service features will be most attractive. You improve the *effectiveness* of your marketing programmes.

Segmentation improves *efficiency* by focusing your marketing spending on the group of people who are most likely to be receptive to your brand message. Every brand has some limited budget for marketing and brand building. That budget might be as small as €3,000 or as large as €300 million – but there is some limit. Segmentation enhances efficiency by peeling away irrelevant (to your brand) people. Segmentation ensures that your limited resources aren't diluted – but directed in a way that yields maximum effect.

Demographics are clearly an important element of targeting. But starting the segmentation process with demographics fails to embrace more fundamental factors that are driving brand choice. People don't buy Volvos because they are "women, 25 to 45 years old". They buy Volvos because safety is the primary criterion in selecting a brand of car. People don't order Heineken because they are "urban, professional males". They order Heineken because they are at happy hour with their work colleagues and want to make a good impression.

In developing a targeting strategy for your brand, first identify market segments – either by profit, by behaviour or by benefit. Determine which segment is best for your brand to focus on. Which segment best aligns with your brand's image? Which segment is not well served by a competitor? After deciding the segment for your brand, describe the segment using demographics. Use demographics for describing segments, not for forming them.

TRUTH

19

Public relations and damage control: the defining moment

The fact is, bad things happen. Quality is left unchecked and E-coli or lead poisoning occur. All of a sudden, a brand's worst nightmare becomes an issue. Brands and companies get scared and utter those two horrible words, "no comment". Now is the time for brands to take the worst possible situation and create the brand's defining moment out of it.

Yes, there are positive PR stories every day, and the value of that third-party endorsement is immeasurable. The angst for brand managers, however, is the handling of the crisis situations. Often seen as serious threats to the life of the brand, negative situations are met with fear. However, when a crisis is confronted head on and put into the perspective of the brand's values, the crisis can be turned into a course-altering, defining moment.

When in a crisis, a brand has, very simply, two choices: face the situation head on or avoid it. Crisis situations that gather media focus usually also cause lawyers to get involved. Legal teams are charged with protecting the company. As such, a recommendation of not commenting on a situation publicly is often standard. From a brand perspective, however, this is dangerous because it allows the media to form its own opinions of the situation.

A company known as Fig, with offices throughout the US, offered women a chance to lose fat through the unproven lipo-dissolve system. In a sudden surprise, it closed all its doors, having lost funding from its investors. The media had been running stories about women who were disappointed in their results. Fig refused to comment on results and its story was not told. Its investors started to hear the concerns, and that, coupled with some other business issues, caused investors to lose confidence and pull all the funding. Perhaps there were no positive results to talk about, but that we will never know.

> When a crisis is confronted head on and put into the perspective of the brand's values, the crisis can be turned into a course-altering, defining moment.

It is difficult to face a crisis head on, acknowledge it and address it in the marketplace – but it works. The quintessential example in the US is Johnson & Johnson and the painkiller Tylenol. Its very public acknowledgement of the tampering issue generated an enormous amount of long-term respect for the company.

In a similar and more recent vein, tainted dog and cat food caused enormous concerns for pet owners throughout the US. Some brands, such as Nestlé Purina and Procter & Gamble's Iams, jumped when they heard this news, pulled product, generated media releases and created sections on their websites for concerned pet owners. Despite the horrible situation, they maintained the trust of the consumers they served because they addressed the issue head on.

Taco Bell went through a significant E-coli scare. A number of stores served the tainted food and within days, Taco Bell had closed nine of its restaurants. The restaurants stayed closed until the problem was isolated, eliminated and the restaurants were safe again for the consumers. During that time, numerous reports went out to keep the public up to date. Taco Bell acted swiftly and, in fact, was complimented during the ordeal by the Chief Medical Officer of the FDA's Center for Food Safety and Applied Nutrition for its cooperative response.

When Taco Bell reopened its doors, the consumers came back. The trust Taco Bell built in the brand provided consumers with confidence that the problems were corrected and the food was safe again – a great example of a bad situation becoming a defining moment because of the actions of the brand.

Bad situations will occur. Some are the direct result of a company, and others occur due to distributors, contract manufacturers and so on. When a crisis situation occurs, the brand must look for the opportunity to create its defining moment. Stand up for values of the brand and share those values with the marketplace through appropriate action. Create a brand opportunity to be known not for what happened, but for the brand's ability to live its values and do the right thing for its consumers.

Stand up for values of the brand and share those values with the marketplace through appropriate action.

TRUTH

20

Focus equals simplicity

Great brands are built on a foundation of simplicity. Simplicity is important for two fundamental reasons. The number of brands and brand messages consumers are exposed to is staggering. And consumers' motivation and ability to process all the information that engulfs their world is limited. Taken together, simplicity is the best hope of gaining the consumer's attention and communicating the meaning of your brand in a very cluttered world.

Although most marketing professionals agree on the importance of simplicity, having the discipline to embrace simplicity can be difficult. Simplicity begins with the message of the brand – and this brand message needs to be focused. Having a focused brand is the first, and perhaps most important, step towards simplicity. However, a focused brand message is not enough. Brand managers must be diligent and refuse to extend the brand to products that are inconsistent with the brand message. Simplicity gets diluted when brands are over-extended. Simplicity gets lost with inconsistent messaging.

Simplicity is the best hope of gaining the consumer's attention and communicating the meaning of your brand in a very cluttered world.

Q-Tip focuses on the very simple concept "cotton swab". Imagine the difficulty of staying focused on that simple concept. Q-Tip managers have resisted the urge to extend the brand into such logical areas as face wipes, ear drops, gauze, cotton balls and so on. By resisting these diversions and staying focused on the cotton bud, Unilever has built a brand that consumers easily understand. Maintaining focus year after year under pressure to "leverage brand equity" actually enhances the value of the brand. Consumers understand what Q-Tip means. This understanding improves the likelihood of Q-Tip being the brand of choice for people looking for a cotton swab.

Consider that a consumer's mind allocates limited space for brands. Consumers will never remember everything, but they must remember enough to choose your particular brand. When it is time to make a purchase, can the consumer easily recall something relevant and distinguishing about your brand? When simplicity is at the heart of your brand essence, the chance of choosing your brand dramatically increases. The less a consumer needs to work to recall and consider your brand, the more likely you are to benefit with a purchase.

When simplicity is at the heart of your brand essence, the chance of choosing your brand dramatically increases.

After all, the last thing you want to do is have your customer work to remember you. Simplicity is the quickest path for a consumer.

Simplicity is not easily attained, however. It requires rigorous understanding of the brand essence and the ability to boil all of the many features and benefits of a brand down to one or two poignant points. On top of it all, once simplicity is achieved, listen for the nay-sayers. "Is that all?" "But that is so simple." "Anyone could have done that it is too easy." Don't be frustrated by such comments. Those comments are, indeed, compliments that the job of identifying the brand essence was done well. The fact of the matter is, achieving simplicity is not easy. Yet, when successfully accomplished, it seems so obvious.

Simplicity is about being direct and focused. Consider the US dessert Jell-O. Watch it wiggle, see it jiggle. The simplicity of a jelly is that it is fun. The advertising, the packaging and the promotions all support this focused brand message. Again, the challenge for Jello's brand team is staying committed to this brand essence. With a product like Jell-O, much like Q-Tips, there are so many options for brand and product proliferation. However, focus and staying true to the simplicity of the brand promise keeps Jell-O a strong and timeless brand.

US supermarket chain Kmart is a great example of a brand that lacked simplicity and, therefore, focus. Kmart began its deep decline a number of years ago. One can argue that its competitors, Wal-Mart and Target, had much to do with its decline. Bul, as you dig deeper, you can see that Wal-Mart stands for inexpensive prices. A simple and focused message. Target stands for great design at value prices. Once again, focused and consistent. But, what can be said for Kmart?

It competed on value for a while. It tried to be the one-stop shop as well. It took a stab at a more designer focus, but for the clothing only, not for the rest of its products. As it shifted its messages, it became anything but simple and focused. It became a muddle. What is a consumer left to do? When an inexpensive item was needed, the top name in the consumer's Rolodex became Wal-Mart. When a stylish item of good value was needed, yes, you're right – Target popped to the top of the consumer's list.

Focus your brand and strive for simplicity. This will connect with consumers. A direct connection with consumers is what makes brands great.

TRUTH

21

Marketing is courtship, not combat

War is often used as a metaphor for marketing. It's not uncommon to view headlines in the business press such as "Texas is Prime Turf in Truck War" or "ExpressJet Adopts Guerilla Marketing". Books such as *Marketing Warfare* continue to reinforce marketing as combat, with discussions of "flanking manoeuvres" and "frontal assaults".

Such thinking is inevitably competitor-focused rather than consumer-focused. After all, war is essentially about destroying or subjugating the competition. Being competitor-focused leads to "me-too" imitation products (if your competition offers this product, you should too), copying strategies (under the assumption that you don't know what you should be doing, but somehow your competitor does) and heavy discounting (often referred to as "price wars"). A competitor-focus encourages a myopic fixation on market share and sales volume rather than profitability, as market share and sales volume are more publicly visible metrics.

This focus on combat perhaps derives from the competitive nature of western society, perhaps from the competitive focus in business school, or perhaps simply from people's natural tendency to compare how they are doing against others. The final arbiter in these battles, though, is the consumer. It is the consumer who "votes". It is through a focus on pleasing the consumer that you encourage the voting to go your way.

Consider the introduction of a new brand of pet food. National sales meetings are big events with at least one objective to generate excitement and enthusiasm among the sales force. One new brand was conceived and designed to specifically target one of the company's primary competitors. The CEOs of these two large companies were well known for their dislike of each other.

Outside the large meeting auditorium, a boxing ring was constructed. During breaks, two kickboxers sparred for the attendees. One kickboxer wore trunks emblazoned with the logo of the new brand, while the other boxer's trunks bore the logo of the competitor brand. The kickboxers battled with the encouragement of the growing crowd. Cheers and applause erupted when, inevitably, the new brand boxer knocked out the other.

The success of a brand comes from the brand's capability to connect with its target audience, to create a compelling product offering and to fundamentally offer a more powerful value proposition.

Such theatrics make for great fun with the sales force. But the success of this brand comes not because of the management's desire to "knock out" the competitor. Rather, the success of this brand comes from the brand's capability to connect with its target audience, to create a compelling product offering and to fundamentally offer a more powerful value proposition.

US brewer SABMiller competes closely with Anheuser-Busch. Miller has run humorous ads aimed at its rival's customers. In one ad, a Dalmatian riding along in a carriage pulled by Clydesdales (visual references to Budweiser mascots) sees a Miller lager truck with "Miller Lite has more taste than Bud Light" on the side. At a red light, the dog makes the leap from the carriage to the cab of the Miller truck. These ads, while very funny, tend to be aimed as much at the competitor as the consumer.

Consider dating as a more appropriate metaphor for marketing. Dating is not about beating up your competition. Dating is about making yourself more attractive (physically, emotionally and intellectually) so that the person whom you are interested in chooses you rather than anyone else.

Successful dating involves getting to know well the person you are interested in. It is creating experiences that highlight your strengths and character, particularly those that will resonate well with desires of the other. If the person you are interested in enjoys cultural activities, an invitation to the theatre will be more enthusiastically received than an invitation to a boxing match. It's not at all about your competitors – it's about who you are and how well you match with the person.

Consider dating as a more appropriate metaphor for marketing.

And, so it should be with your brand. Consider your target audience. Market research can provide insight into their needs and how they see your brand. How can you make your brand more attractive? Advertising, price, packaging, distribution channel, personal selling, publicity, promotion, product or service features all can work to woo your target audience.

Advertising can create an appealing personality around your brand, such as it has for BMW's Mini Cooper. Distribution decisions such as the type of retailers that will carry your brand can enhance its attractiveness. Whether your brand is sold through Harrod's or Lidl affects its attractiveness. Either can be appropriate – it depends on with whom you are trying to connect.

Don't ignore your competition. However, first and foremost, keep your eye on your consumer. By creating your brand as more attractive, demand will move in your direction. Importantly, this demand is not the result of what you have done to your competition, but rather what you have done for your consumer. Marketing is more courtship than combat.

TRUTH

22

Don't sacrifice brand focus for sales

Many brands become successful through clear focus on a particular attribute or benefit that is meaningful to their target customers. These brands typically show good sales growth when awareness of the brand and its attractive features draws in those people who find some affinity with the brand. Eventually, the brand reaches saturation – as appealing as the brand is to a particular group, there is always some natural limit to the sales potential.

When faced with slowing sales growth, management, with typical can-do spirit, seeks ways to continue growth. Such efforts often lead to expanding the appeal of the brand by moving it away from its well-defined focus.

The Saturn car company built a great brand based upon a unique no-hassle, friendly sales experience. Additionally, the models were all small, relatively inexpensive and utilitarian. Saturn appealed to younger, practical and economically-minded car buyers in the US. This strategy created a distinctive image for the Saturn brand and differentiated it from other competitors, which had become increasingly indistinguishable.

> As appealing as the brand is to a particular group, there is always some natural limit to the sales potential.

Over time, Saturn's growth slowed down and management began to look for ways to expand the brand. Often Saturn owners would trade out of the brand as they grew older and improved their economic status. The undeniable logic was to introduce a more upmarket model to provide Saturn owners with a trade-up option. The Saturn LS was larger, more luxurious and more expensive than the other models – in other words, the opposite of what Saturn was known for.

The Saturn LS did not do particularly well. Not because it was not a good car, but because it was not consistent with the focus Saturn had built. Saturn's new convertible, Sky, seems to be a good addition to the Saturn line – attractive, small and relatively inexpensive.

The entire concept of brand extensions centres on this very issue: whether to stay focused with a brand or extend a brand into new areas to build sales volume. Organisations couch this in marketing speak such as "we need to leverage the brand". At the heart of the matter is: do you make changes to your brand that may affect its long-term viability to achieve short-term sales?

Don't sacrifice the health of your brand for short-term sales gains.

The answer is no. Don't sacrifice the health of your brand for short-term sales gains. Although it may help with meeting this quarter's numbers, expanding or changing the focus of a brand will cause long-term brand damage. That type of damage is hard to quantify and even harder to correct.

Consider the retailer The Limited, once a popular clothing chain for young American women. The Limited helped to usher in new looks in fashion at reasonable prices. Contemporary and stylish, it had an enormous following among teens and young adults. But, as sales pressures increased, and to meet opportunity beyond its current target audience, The Limited changed to meet the pressure of the current sales quotas. As a result of the shift in brand focus, the styles weren't quite as snazzy – they didn't meet the needs of the contemporary market. Additionally, it tried to extend its reach beyond its original target audience. It didn't take long before it wasn't clear what the brand truly stood for in the market. The Limited as a retail chain is all but defunct now. But, the lessons still strongly apply. Expanding a brand beyond its capabilities to achieve short-term sales can, in some cases, destroy a brand.

Starbucks' same-store sales and share price have been declining. In a move to strengthen its core coffee business, Starbucks is discontinuing hot breakfast sandwiches. Starbucks makes great coffee – and this is the source of its profits. Leave the breakfast sandwiches to someone else.

Expanding a brand beyond its capabilities to drive additional sales is most tempting when the brand is doing exceptionally well. With Saturn, or The Limited, or any other hip, cool and "in" brand, when performance is strong, the brand seems invincible. That, of course, is the exact point in time when the brand manager must take a strong stand to protect the integrity of the brand. That is also when energy is high and executives are convinced that much can be done to squeeze more volume out of a brand. It is precisely at that time, however, that you need to be vigilant so that the meaning of the brand is not sacrificed in the chase for sales.

Focusing on the long run is not always easy in highly competitive corporate cultures. However, too much emphasis on short-term sales increases can erode the value of the brand, causing larger problems down the road.

TRUTH

23

The medium is not
the message; the message
is the message

The Super Bowl is the perennial clash of NFL division winners. It has also become the Super Bowl of advertising. Advertisers bid on air time so that their brand is part of this media event. In recent years, Super Bowl thirty-second spots have commanded in the neighbourhood of $2.5 million. Yes, you read that right – $2.5 million for 30 seconds of air time.

Advertisers use those few seconds to try to create images and ideas that will enter the national psyche. However, many have failed. These ads were missing a compelling message. They were forgettable adverts whose greatest fame was their Super Bowl appearance.

Advertisers pay premium rates to be a part of an event – the Olympics, the final episode of *Friends* and so on – believing that, in addition to a large audience, associating with such an event bestows stature, prestige and significance. But without a compelling message, such spending satisfies only the company's marketing department, advertising agency and perhaps the ego of the CEO.

To justify the expense, media experts will argue that the reach is so great with these events that they are worth the cost. But is reach the only thing that matters? There is no denying that it is important to reach your target audience. However, media experts know that it is a combination of reach (getting to your target) and frequency (the number of times your target sees and hears the message) that creates awareness of and favourability towards your brand. In other words, seeing something once is not enough. In this cluttered world, people need to see, hear and experience advertising messages many times before becoming aware of the brand and forming individual impressions of the brand.

Prime-time television reaches a large audience but at significant expense. In the US Pontiac has decided to forgo this costly medium,

> Without a compelling message, such spending satisfies only the company's marketing department, advertising agency and perhaps the ego of the CEO.

and instead focus on less glamorous, but better targeted media that will better reach its target of younger drivers.

With major media opportunities such as the final *Pop Idol* show of the year, you get reach, but what about frequency? No doubt, millions will view your ad one time during the *Pop Idol* finale. But, is it worth the cost for one exposure? The medium is nothing more than that – a medium for delivering your message.

The Academy Awards is another major event for advertisers. The advertisers and audience, of course, are a bit different from the Super Bowl. Revlon, L'Oreal and other cosmetic and fashion designers frequently advertise at enormous cost. But, when it is all said and done, what do people remember? Viewers of the Academy Awards may tell you what designer gown Nicole Kidman wore or which shoes Cameron Diaz chose for the evening. But, they may have a hard time remembering the messages of Revlon.

The medium is nothing more than that – a medium for delivering your message.

Perhaps the genesis of medium as message or of Super-Bowl-as-advertising-event was the introduction of the Apple Macintosh in 1984. The commercial portrayed a young woman fleeing "thought police" as she propelled a large hammer towards a large video screen, smashing an image of Big Brother. This widely anticipated spot launched Macintosh as the irreverent alternative to the dominating IBM PC.

Although the Super Bowl helped Apple introduce its revolutionary computer to a huge audience, it was the message, not the medium, that differentiated Macintosh from its primary competitor – a message reinforced over the years across many media. Many consumers have developed a passion for Macintosh not because it advertised on the Super Bowl, but because of the symbolic image the advertising created.

Ego can get wrapped up quite a bit with these media. For companies that are committed to their brands, for individuals who support the efforts of the company, regardless of their role in the organisation, it is with pride that they announce during a Super Bowl party, "Look for our ad; we tried to get it in the first quarter." When it is a leader of the organisation whose ego is helping to drive the decision to make a Super Bowl or *Pop Idol* final show media buy, it is all the more difficult for the brand manager to articulate the lack of benefits in investing in the medium rather than the message. Facts should trump emotional business decisions any day. But, when ego is involved, that is a difficult challenge.

The medium for a message can be alluring – reaching millions, and generating prestige, stature and significance to the brands that participate. It can be thrilling to be part of a significant event. But, the role of the medium is to deliver a message. Ultimately, the medium is not the message – the message is the message.

TRUTH

24

Brand development and the small business

Small businesses face particular challenges. Small businesses can face tighter cash flow, tougher access to capital, smaller budgets and fewer specialised personnel. Often, people working at a small business are expected to take on several roles – for some of which they may not be ideally trained.

The competitive marketplace does not, however, give small businesses a free pass. Small businesses face the same market challenges as their larger counterparts – how best to differentiate, who is the ideal customer and what is the core meaning of the brand. Addressing these fundamental brand development questions is just as important, if not more so, for the small business.

St Louis grocer Straub's has only four stores but understands well the importance of differentiation and focus. The grocery market is highly competitive with large chains like Schnucks, discount grocers Aldi's and Save-a-Lot, and speciality grocers such as Trader Joe's, Whole Foods and Wild Oats.

Straub's secures a profitable spot in this challenging landscape through adhering to fundamental brand-building principles. It starts with a clear understanding of the type of customer that it wants to build its business around – higher income, professional, educated and discerning. The rest of its business flows from there.

> Small businesses face the same market challenges as their larger counterparts.

It locates its stores perfectly to match its target customers – stores in affluent neighbourhoods. It's hard to differentiate on basic products – Heinz ketchup and Bounty paper towels are pretty much the same regardless of where one buys them. Straub's does, though, provide notably higher-quality fruit and vegetables. Professional butchers are immediately accessible to serve up any of the store's excellent meats or explain how long a two-pound beef tenderloin should be cooked. An extensive deli offers selections of fully prepared or partially prepared high-quality items perfect for busy professionals. The wine selection is extensive and tailored to the tastes of its customer base. Straub's responds to special orders and offers its own store account for payment. Regardless of how busy the store seems, checkout is magically quick and simple – lanes open up to accommodate departing customers. Straub's management has created a complete experience that is very attractive – not to everyone, but to a particular type of customer. By successfully differentiating in a way that is meaningful to higher-end customers, Straub's also has greater pricing flexibility and the capability to generate profits in a tough industry.

Differentiating in a new market means developing a new and distinctive brand, as shown by AMS Controls, a family-owned US business that specialised in making controllers that regulate and manage roll-forming machines. By focusing on this particular business, AMS Controls had developed credibility and a good reputation among both roll-forming machine manufacturers and end users. As it turned out, the technology and software that control roll-forming machines can be adapted to control metal-folding machines. AMS Controls began work on developing expertise in this application area and created a highly competent controller for metal-folding machines.

AMS Controls had a good product for the metal-folding market but faced two significant branding challenges. First, it was not known in the metal-folding market. Metal-folding machine manufacturers, primarily located in Europe, weren't familiar with them. End users, unless they also operated roll-forming machines, also weren't familiar with AMS Controls. Second, AMS Controls did not want to risk diluting the strong association that it had built between its brand and roll-forming expertise.

So AMS Controls developed a completely new brand name for its metal-folding controller. By developing a completely separate name, it keeps AMS Controls associated just on roll forming and gives the new brand an opportunity to build its own unique reputation in the folding machine controller market.

AMS Controls, like many technology-based companies, had a (bad) habit of naming its products with letters and numbers (such as its XL200 Series Controller). For this new product, AMS Controls wanted a brand name that had some inherent meaning to its potential customers in the metal-folding market. It chose the name Pathfinder because it captured the key benefit of the software embedded in the controller. The software will take any finished product and determine the optimal path through the metal-bending machine to minimise bends, speeding production and limiting waste.

With a solid product and a new brand name, it introduced Pathfinder to the metal-folding market through some of the basic marketing tactics proven effective in this industry – trade shows, product brochures, product demonstration and personal selling.

Family-owned Corley Printing Company takes great pride in mastery of its craft. Although it has always been passionate about its business, it has recently explored ways to communicate that passion in very visible and tangible ways. Its car park has been repainted. In lieu of parking spots marked with typical straight lines and curbs painted in traditional yellow, Corley painted press sheet registration marks to indicate the parking spaces and painted its curbs with the printing process colours (cyan, magenta, yellow and black). People in the design and reproduction industry will instantly recognise these unique markings – and a simple thing like a car park is transformed into an expression of passion for the business.

The keys to building a strong brand for small businesses are the same basic principles employed by successful larger brands.

The Straub's, AMS Controls and Corley Printing Company examples illustrate that the keys to building a strong brand for small businesses are the same basic principles employed by successful larger brands – be clear on your target, develop meaningful differentiation, have a name that reflects something important about your brand, avoid brand extension, communicate brand passion and design your marketing activity and brand experience to be relevant to your target customer.

TRUTH

25

Imitation is an ineffective form of flattery

Everyone loves success. And people love to imitate those who are successful – to drive the same model car that their favourite footballer drives, to carry the same bag as a model, or to mimic the hairstyle of a famous actress. Business people read books like Jack Welch's *Jack: Straight from the Gut* hoping to duplicate his leadership success.

Benchmarking is simply another popular variant on imitation. You measure your competition's performance on relevant attributes and meet (or slightly beat) their performance. Think of this as *imitative incrementalism*. You'll be just like your competitor (but a little better). Such strategy rarely leads to strong brands but rather to me-too brands with points of difference that are relevant to the company but not to consumers.

Pepsi One is a brand that has been struggling. The "One" refers to one calorie – as distinct from diet soft drinks that have zero calories. Although the meaningfulness of "one" versus "zero" calories seems elusive, Pepsi One's disappointing performance stems from a strategic marketing failure – imitation rather than differentiation.

Pepsi One's introductory advertising featured people on a rocking boat, with some drinking Coke and some drinking Pepsi One. As the boat rocked back and forth, the cans would shift from person to person. People were alternating sips of Coke and sips of Pepsi One without ever noticing the difference. This was Pepsi One's "big idea" – it tastes just like Coke.

Well, if people wanted something that tasted just like Coke, wouldn't they just order a Coke? Pepsi One is destined to follow a line of failed extensions (Crystal Pepsi, Pepsi A.M. and so on) because Pepsi failed to establish a meaningful point of difference. Imitation may be the sincerest form of flattery, but it doesn't drive sales.

One of the most successful US airlines today is Southwest Airlines. During a time that saw the demise through bankruptcy or merger of brands such as Pan Am and TWA, a small airline born in Texas grew into one of the few consistently profitable air carriers. Success came because of its novel approach to the business. Southwest trimmed amenities to offer lower fares to a segment of the market that valued price over a warmed-up chicken and rice dinner. Southwest served smaller airports with lower overheads. It flew only one model of jet to keep maintenance and training costs down.

Even companies with the clout of Microsoft can't overcome insufficient differentiation.

Wisely not focusing solely on price, Southwest hired enthusiastic, friendly flight attendants. Rather than putting them in the traditional navy blue suits so common in the industry, Southwest dressed its attendants in casual khaki outfits. Southwest focused on differentiating its brand in a way meaningful to its target customer.

Southwest's success has not gone unnoticed. Several of the traditional major carriers introduced brands designed to imitate Southwest's success. Both Continental and Delta attempted some version of the low-cost fun ethos of Southwest Airlines. Although the failure of each was certainly due to a host of contributing factors, a fundamental failure to differentiate was certainly one reason.

Apple's iPod is far and away the dominant MP3 player. An early entrant to the market, blessed with Apple's superb design sense, ease of use, and coupled with iTunes, the iPod quickly became a hit. Creative Technologies and Microsoft developed their own versions of the iPod. Branded Zen and Zune respectively, neither has captured the imagination of the consumer nor seen great market success. Neither brought significant differentiation to their brand. Some of each were sold, no question, but neither offered people a strong and compelling reason to choose them over iPod. Even companies with the clout of Microsoft can't overcome insufficient differentiation.

Imitators often fail because they don't (or can't) imitate the full magical mix of their target brand. Sure, they can dress their flight attendants in khaki, but have they created a culture that reinforces fun and enthusiasm? Yes, they've benchmarked hardware specs, but is their product as elegantly designed?

Imitators often fail because they don't (or can't) imitate the full magical mix of their target brand.

Another reason imitators often fail is that they lost the powerful first-mover advantage. Innovative brands that are first in their market benefit from early association as a leader, the expert. Making inroads against these brands requires meaningful differentiation.

Finding your brand's differentiation is not necessarily easy – research, intuition, analysis and creative insight can all help. Sometimes luck can make the difference. To set up your brand for best success, though, requires differentiation, not imitation.

TRUTH

26

Positioning lives in the mind of your target customer

Where does a brand exist? Does Tide exist in a particular place in a shop? No, because that is where Tide the product (rather than Tide the brand) can be found. Does Starbucks exist on streets in big cities? No, because that is where Starbucks the service is created. These are important differences.

Brand managers often think they own the brand – that they control it. Brand managers, however, are charged with creating experiences that can solidify the message of the brand, the position of the brand in the consumer's mind. This can be startling for brand managers who want to feel a sense of complete control over their brand's positioning.

As a result, it is all the more important that a brand manager creates a total experience around a brand position through exceptionally consistent messaging. All the experiential factors, when done in a consistent manner, can help to infuse the customer's mind with clarity around the brand position. It seems obvious but is often forgotten or taken for granted. However, implicit in this idea of consistency is that the brand as a product or service must perform in a manner consistent with the messaging being delivered. There is no greater way to destroy a position in a consumer's mind than to have the brand not deliver as promised.

A brand exists in the mind of the consumer. And it is here that the brand struggles to find a foothold. Finding a foothold – getting the brand lodged somewhere in the brain – is the first step. The second step is building meaningful associations (images, facts) around the brand. Guinness the brand exists in our mind within a network of related concepts (tradition, Ireland, black and white, and so on).

The brand team does not fully control the position the brand has; they merely influence it.

Building these associations requires taking actions consistent with principles of cognitive psychology and learning. Keep your brand message simple – because relatively inattentive minds can more easily process simple information. Be consistent over time – such consistency reinforces the link between your brand and other concepts you intend to associate with your brand.

Head and Shoulders shampoo has stayed true to the same simple concept – it helps treat dandruff – year after year. In doing so, the brand has established itself in the consumer's mind as associated with dandruff control.

But what if management suggests that a particular brand needs to grow another two share points the following year? The focus of the brand then feels confining. A natural inclination is to expand the meaning of the brand so that more market share can be achieved. But the brand team does not fully control the position the brand has; they merely influence it. Trying to expand a brand's position typically leads to confusion in a marketplace, not additional sales. So, to obtain the growth goals, just the opposite must occur. Tighter focus on a brand and stronger consistency in messaging can all help the brand to be more alive for the consumer, with share gains then to follow. Unfortunately, however, this is counter-intuitive.

Have you ever visited an American Girl store? Do you know a young girl who is amazingly enamoured with her American Girl doll? Every experience and every touch point that a child has with this brand reinforces the brand message. The position statement for American Girl probably addresses sense of self, being true to your identity and valuing the difference that outstanding girls have.

Flip through an American Girl catalogue and you see stories about the dolls, the lives they lead and the activities they prefer. Your trip to an American Girl store is not complete without a stop at the tea room, where the young girl in your life has lunch or tea with their doll in

> Tighter focus on a brand and stronger consistency in messaging can all help the brand to be more alive for the consumer.

a highchair at the table. During lunch, you might check out the cards that are conversation starters, with questions such as: "What one thing would you want to change about yourself?" The American Girl brand connects with self-esteem for young girls.

For a seven-year-old girl with such a doll, the brand will undoubtedly live very clearly in her mind. American Girl, the brand organisation, does a fabulous job of creating experiences and products that continually reinforce that very position in the mind of their target.

What does your brand mean – not in your mind, but in the mind of your consumer?

Brand managers create the position statement. They define where the brand should exist in the target's mind. But, ultimately, the only thing they can truly control are the various messages and experiences regarding the brand. The brand position does not live with the brand manager – it lives with the target audience.

TRUTH

27

The value of brand loyalty

Loyal customers are an important brand asset. Loyal customers represent a profit stream paying out over the years. This notion is referred to as "customer lifetime value" and is predicated on loyal customers representing a stream of revenue (and profit) over time. In some businesses, the value of a customer can be quantified by projecting expected revenue, costs (including acquisition and retention costs) and likelihood of retention over time. The lifetime value of customers can be increased by any combination of increasing revenue from that customer, reducing costs and increasing retention rate.

Improving customer loyalty benefits both revenues and costs. Loyal customers generate more revenue in several ways. First, they tend to be less price sensitive – attracted to your brand for reasons other than price. Loyal customers give a greater share of their business in that category to your brand. (A loyal Crest toothpaste user might buy Crest 80% of the time, whereas a less loyal user might choose Crest only 30% of the time.) Customer revenue may also increase over time. Real estate agents (earning commissions) who nurture loyal clients will see their earnings grow as their clients trade up (buy and sell) increasingly to larger, more expensive homes. Loyal customers may also become brand advocates, generating positive word of mouth and thereby indirectly generating additional revenue via referrals.

> Loyal customers represent a profit stream paying out over the years.

Higher customer loyalty also helps on the cost side. Loyal customers with more experience with your brand typically will be more efficient to service. For customers returning again and again to the same printing company, there will be a history of working together and understanding of expectations and procedures that simply makes doing business together easier. Loyal customers will need less post-sale support. For example, loyal Microsoft Office customers, with years of experience with the brand, will need less technical support.

Consider the simple example of a US residential heating and cooling company, Morgner Air Conditioning and Heating. Morgner fields a number of service technicians but prefers to have the same technician consistently service the same house. It is not unusual for a Morgner technician to service the same house across two, three or four different owners. New owners will be inclined to continue with Morgner since they have experience with that house's systems. Morgner benefits because the servicing technician has years of experience at that particular location and knows the history and quirks of that particular system. Morgner offers attractive service packages over several years – an easy choice for satisfied customers. Loyalty can work well for both parties.

In considering loyalty for your brand, it is important to distinguish behavioural loyalty from attitudinal loyalty. Behavioural loyalty is simply repeatedly buying a brand – regardless of the reasons behind that purchasing behaviour. Attitudinal loyalty is an affection, a good emotional feeling and a sense of commitment to a brand.

Drawing this distinction is important because one can sometimes misinterpret behavioural loyalty for attitudinal loyalty. Large department stores often rely heavily on special sales – with several

Loyalty can work well for both parties.

weekends a month often featuring a themed sale. Tracking customer purchase activity could reveal a large number of loyal customers – but "loyal" only because they buy discounted merchandise during sales periods, not loyal out of a genuine commitment to that retailer. That's not to say that there aren't people with an underlying loyalty to these retailers – just that you can't always discern this from simply looking at purchase behaviour over time.

A great example of attitudinal loyalty is a recent commercial for the Porsche 911. A boy gazing out of a classroom window sees a 911 drive by. After school, he rides his bike to the local dealership. All of about 11 years old, he asks to see the new 911. He sits in the car, barely able to see over the steering wheel. Getting out of the car, he asks the salesperson for a business card and says, "Thanks, I'll see you in about twenty years." The voice-over announcer says, "It's a funny thing about a Porsche. There's the moment you know you first want one. There's the moment you first own one. And for the truly afflicted, there's the decade or two that passes in between." When that 11-year-old boy returns twenty years from now, you can be sure it will be because of strong affection for the brand, not because of some special sale.

Strong brands have a customer base that wants to associate with the brand not because it is the cheapest or deluges them with special incentives, but rather because the brand provides value to their lives. Brands with a meaningful point of difference, brands that make an emotional connection with customers, and brands that foster *attitudinal* loyalty, promote loyalty not because of discounts they offer their customers – these are bribes for business – but because the brand represents something their customers are proud of. These brands are earning, not buying, loyalty. How is your brand achieving loyalty?

TRUTH

28

Quality is not an effective branding message

Quality is a great statement to make about your brand. It is even better when your customers make that statement about your brand for you. Yet, having a quality product or service is not the end of branding efforts, but only the beginning. Quality just gets you in the game and brings your brand into consideration. Brands that are not delivering a quality product or service consistent with their price will disappear (think of the Yugo!).

Attention to quality is fine. Marketing managers get into trouble, though, when they believe that quality is the basis on which their brand competes in the marketplace. Brand managers too focused on a quality message send their brand adrift without much meaning.

"Our brand is the quality leader," they might say.

Or "our customers buy our product because of its quality", you may sometimes hear.

All of this may be true. But what business openly proclaims to have a shoddy product or mediocre services? Sure, Boeing builds quality planes...but then so does Airbus. Anheuser-Busch is definitely an excellent brewery...but so is SABMiller. This abstract notion of quality doesn't go far in differentiating brands. It can be difficult for brand managers to see clearly that their competitors' offerings are often of quality similar to their own.

If you and your competitor both offer a quality product (as is likely the case), why should someone choose your brand rather than your competitor's? What meaningful point of difference do you offer? What emotional connection have you made? What unique imagery have you built around your brand? Heinz is not the only company to make quality ketchup. Heinz, however, has created a point of difference with "thick".

Quality means different things to different people. For some, a quality watch may mean "rugged"; for others, it may mean "accurate"; and for still others, it may mean "high status". Quality is an abstract concept referring to many different dimensions of a brand's performance. An effective positioning is tangible, clear and

Quality means different things to different people.

concrete. Concepts such as "fast", "reliable", "fun", "youthful" and "safe" vividly portray the benefit delivered by a brand.

Quality is expected in a brand.

Quality is expected in a brand. Although the level of quality expectations varies by price (you expect a £400 DVD player to be of a higher "quality" than a £100 DVD player), consumers fundamentally expect a quality product. Most companies are operating consistently with basic consumer expectations around quality. (If not, they aren't in business long!)

"Quality" doesn't *differentiate* brands. The Nissan Navara, Mini Cooper, Honda Civic and Lexus LS460 are all "quality" cars. But simply noting they are all quality cars does nothing to reflect the different experiences each provides. The Honda Civic delivers on basic reliable transportation. The Mini Cooper represents a fun small car. The Lexus LS range promises "a high performance saloon". Each of these brands has its distinctiveness and is aimed at different people. "Quality" does nothing to reflect these differences and distinguish these brands from each other.

Why be so vigilant about avoiding quality as a branding message? Because it is so easy to fall back on. Positioning your brand's key message is a critical branding decision. Choosing an effective positioning requires making a tough choice from among several good alternatives. Should a bank position on low rates? Should a bank position on individualised personal service? What about accessible ATMs? Or perhaps simplified e-banking?

Each one of those positioning alternatives will have its detractors. It is bad to compete on price. Personalised service will be too expensive to deliver and isn't a key decision criterion for 55% of bank customers. Accessible ATMs as a positioning seems so 1990s. Positioning on e-banking doesn't create the right emotional bond with customers...and on and on. Inevitably someone will suggest positioning the bank on quality. How can anyone object to that? It sounds great and fits perfectly with the bank's mission and vision statements. But what does it really mean?

Quality in manufacturing is important. Quality in customer service is important. Having customers view your brand as providing good quality for the money is important. Quality is a way to be. It is not a branding message. Your branding message should communicate your brand's special uniqueness.

Quality is a way to be. It's not a branding message.

People need some reason to nudge their choice towards your brand. Quality is necessary for your brand to be considered, but it is not sufficient to warrant a purchase.

TRUTH

29

Effective use of celebrity endorsers: the fit's the thing

Pairing brands with celebrities is a time-honoured tradition (Mark Twain promoted flour in the late 1800s) and continues as popular practice. Top celebrity endorsers are not cheap, however. Catherine Zeta-Jones landed a $20 million T-Mobile agreement; Angelina Jolie signed on with St. John and Nicole Kidman with Chanel, each for $12 million. This shows how expensive such deals can be.

But are these high-priced spokespeople worth it? Do celebrities add value to brands? With smart strategy – possibly.

Celebrities can create caché around a brand. Budweiser Select, an expensive, urban brand, employed popular singer Jay-Z to give the brand a heightened sense of cool. Budweiser Select created a TV commercial featuring Jay-Z and racing driver Dale Earnhardt, Jr, together in an exotic supercar, chasing female racing driver Danica Patrick in a similarly fast car around the streets of Monaco. Using these contemporary celebrities (in addition to an equally cool venue) imbued Budweiser Select with a great sense of panache.

Effectively using a celebrity requires carefully matching the brand with the appropriate celebrity.

Celebrities can create caché around a brand.

Brett Favre and Peyton Manning, two top NFL quarterbacks, served as endorsers for different brands. Peyton Manning appeared in MasterCard commercials, giving "pep talks" directly to the viewer. The Manning moments covered "regular guy" issues such as driving a minivan or starting a new job. These were very funny but seemed to have no meaningful connection to MasterCard. Brett Favre, on the other hand, was featured in a low-key commercial for Wrangler. In the ad, Favre, wearing Wrangler jeans, played a game of touch football with friends. The ad emphasised the comfort of the jeans. Favre was a great choice because his casual working man image is a nice fit with the image of Wrangler. The brand (Wrangler), the celebrity (Favre) and the key message (comfort) fit together seamlessly.

Omega watches has consistently used celebrities in support of its brand. The print ads are all simple, focusing on just the watch on the endorser. Omega's choice of celebrities – Formula One great Michael Schumacher, Olympic swimming stars Ian Thorpe and Michael Phelps, and golfer Sergio Garcia – all reinforce the performance image of the brand. Omega lists on its website "James Bond" as one of its endorsers – a relationship that has been enduring

Effectively using a celebrity requires carefully matching the brand with the appropriate celebrity.

and has transcended the various actors that have played the Bond character. Consistent use over time helps strengthen the relationship between the celebrity and the brand.

US discount insurance carrier Geico's use of celebrities seems odd. A series of commercials feature regular Geico customers along with celebrities such as Charo, Burt Bacharach, Peter Frampton and the Pips. The only common theme seems to be "past their prime". The ads make no obvious connections between the brand's selling message and the celebrity. Possibly the choice of celebrities from the '60s, '70s and '80s reflects Geico's intended target audience; however, Geico's other ads with an animated gecko and cavemen seem to suggest a younger audience that would not connect well with the older celebrities.

Avoid using celebrities who are saturated with other endorsement deals, and be careful about celebrities already strongly associated with another brand. Tiger Woods has had endorsement deals with Nike, American Express, consulting firm Accenture, Tag Heuer watches and Gatorade. Tiger's extensive product endorsement portfolio, in addition to his particularly close association with Nike, made Buick's investment in him as its endorser somewhat questionable. It is difficult to see a natural fit between Tiger and Buick.

Jerry Seinfeld is not overcommitted as an endorser, but he is closely linked with American Express. Seinfeld brings his brand of humour to shopping with American Express. This tight association between Seinfeld and American Express might have limited the effectiveness of Hewlett-Packard's use of Jerry Seinfeld in its campaign. The ads were an extension of HP's campaign that featured celebrities talking about their use of its computers. As the celebrities talked, they made reinforcing motions with their hands that created visual effects that brought to life what they are talking about. Seinfeld's monologue for HP coupled with the reinforcing visual effects work well, as they tie into things associated with Jerry Seinfeld (New York City, diners and so on). However, Jerry Seinfeld is likely to remain most closely associated with American Express.

One important word of caution should be noted here regarding a risk in using celebrities to pitch for your brand – bad celebrity behaviour can be bad for your brand. Chanel and Burberry jettisoned endorser Kate Moss when pictures of her snorting cocaine surfaced. Nike quickly backed out of their relationship with American football player Michael Vick as a result of Vick's involvement with dog fighting. Don't let a tarnished celebrity tarnish your brand.

Celebrity endorsers can be a significant investment for a brand. Make sure the celebrity is a good fit with the brand image. Make sure you can build a strong link between the celebrity and the brand. Make sure the celebrity is relevant to your brand's selling message.

30

Brand-building consumer promotion

Consumer promotions encompass a wide range of activity. Frequent flyer programmes – consumer promotion. Coupons in the Sunday paper – consumer promotion. Contests and sweepstakes – consumer promotion. Holiday sales, rebates, buy-one-get-one-free offers, special trial sizes – yes, all consumer promotions. Effectively using consumer promotions requires clarity around objectives, clarity around the target audience and clarity around brand meaning.

Too often consumer promotions are used simply to temporarily boost sales. These promotions are typically bland coupon programmes. Yet, there is so much more to an effective promotion. To be successful, the objective of the promotion must be clearly defined.

Promotions are designed to stimulate consumer behaviour. As such, there are two fundamental behaviours that promotions attempt to shape. The first behaviour is trial. The intent is to engage consumers and persuade them to try the brand for the first time. Price reductions, sampling, coupons and gifts with purchase are some of the more common trial programmes.

Repeat programmes are the main tools for encouraging and rewarding loyalty. They are designed to encourage a consumer to purchase more of a brand, with the expectation that with repeated good experiences, the consumer will become loyal. In-package coupons, BOGOFs (buy one get one free), bonus packs (more product for the same price) and frequent user cards are all common repeat programmes.

> To be successful, the objective of the promotion must be clearly defined.

McDonald's Monopoly game is a successful repeat programme. The collection of Monopoly pieces encourages consumers to return to McDonald's. Many of the smaller prizes in the Monopoly game bring customers back to McDonald's for a free drink or free order of fries. Heartland milk was trying to make inroads against its chief competitor, Oberweis Dairy, at a local upmarket grocers. Heartland was priced a bit less and needed to reassure potential customers that its milk was as good as Oberweis. Heartland brought into this retailer someone to pour small samples of its various milk products – whole, semi-skimmed and chocolate – for grocery shoppers. Both McDonald's and Heartland were very clear about their objectives.

> A clear understanding of your target audience is also important to effective consumer promotion.

A clear understanding of your target audience is also important to effective consumer promotion. Coupon flyers in Sunday papers can deliver many millions of coupons. Per cent redemption rates often hover in the single digits. Many of these coupons reach people who have no real interest in the featured brand. Price discounting may attract some new consumers (often least-loyal price shoppers) and reduce your margin from loyal customers who would buy your brand anyway. Is this really the best way to reach your target audience?

Thoughtful and creative promotions reduce such waste by focusing promotional funding in a way that connects most directly with the brand's target audience. All start with a clear portrait of the person with whom the brand strives to connect. An autograph session in a shopping centre with a football star may be effective at attracting mothers bringing their children, but probably not so effective at drawing higher-income professional men.

Vespa has been actively rejuvenating and updating its brand of scooters. The company is creating more of a hip, contemporary, young, urban and upmarket image for its brand. Vespa has been strategically displaying scooters in retail establishments that fit well with a particular target audience. A Vespa was on display in Starbucks – but not all Starbucks. This particular Starbucks was located in a younger, professional and affluent area. Vespas were also on display in a Mark Shale clothing store – a clothing store that attracts a predominately professional, well-off, male shopper.

Starbucks and Mark Shale were not Vespa sales locations – rather, they were places for promoting the awareness of Vespa and transferring the image of these retailers to enhance a good impression of the brand. Vespa clearly understands its target audience – and its promotional activity reflects this understanding.

Consumer promotion can also be used to reinforce the brand's positioning. Breitling has been producing high-end timepieces for nearly 120 years. The brand has been built around an association with the aviation industry. Rather than use consumer promotion to discount the price of its watches (and risk devaluing the brand), Breitling's emphasis is on strengthening its positioning. Breitling sponsors the Breitling Master Cup, an international aviation competition. The first successful nonstop around-the-world balloon flight was made by Brian Jones and Bertrand Piccard in the Breitling Orbiter 3. Along these lines, Marlboro provided consumers with an opportunity to save product proof of purchase codes to redeem for items from a western-theme catalogue. This promotion nicely reinforced the brand's positioning.

Keep in mind that although consumer promotions have a role in brand building, they cannot replace advertising as a tool for developing strong associations around your brand. Marketing expenditures have increasingly shifted from advertising to promotion due to an emphasis on short-term, immediate results. Marketing managers like consumer promotions because the effects are quick, visible and tangible. But don't believe that your consumer promotions are having the same effect as an enduring advertising campaign. Let your consumer promotion be a complement to your advertising – not a replacement for it.

TRUTH

31

Advertising built for
the long run

Your advertising campaign's job is to create brand meaning. Repeated over time, your advertising forges a link between your brand and some key benefit or feature. Michelin's use of a baby in a tyre reinforces the idea of trust. Associating with sports communicates "youth" and "high energy" for Lucozade and Red Bull.

Using advertising to build long-term value in a brand is not a sprint – it is a marathon. It requires patience. It requires focus. It requires commitment.

Most importantly, it requires executions with legs. It requires a creative idea, reflecting a single-minded strategy, which can be extended for years. Advertising relying too heavily on clever execution rather than connecting with consumers around a simple selling idea is a one-shot wonder. Perhaps it gets your attention. Perhaps it makes you laugh. But has it really enhanced your affinity for the brand?

> Using advertising to build long-term value in a brand is not a sprint – it is a marathon.

Anheuser-Busch produces some of the funniest advertising on air. Spuds Mackenzie was the ultimate "party animal". There was the guy always trying to get his friends' Bud Light by fruitlessly proclaiming "I love you, man". Frankie and Louie were the wackiest lizards to grace the airwaves. Four young black men had everyone wondering "whazzup?". You have to love the ads with guys using the word "dude" to express five or six ideas depending on how they say "dude". All very funny. But what does its have to do with building a consistent, enduring and meaningful image for Budweiser or Bud Light? "Bud Light – isn't that the brand with all the funny commercials?" is not the most compelling strategic message. To this end, Anheuser-Busch recently stated a need to include more messaging along with the humour in their ads – a move that should serve them well.

The Economist, the business and political weekly with a global perspective, has run a series of simple print ads. These basic ads featured just the brand name with a bold line such as "Think someone under the table", "Lose the ability to slip out of meetings unnoticed" and "Leave no answer unquestioned". In the UK, the adverts are so recognisable that no logo is used, just a consistent red background. These ads deliver a sound, strategic message that *The Economist* provides deep analysis of issues important to our times. "Think someone under the table" is a nice play on the more common expression that begins with "drink". "Lose the ability to slip out of meetings unnoticed" speaks directly to how *The Economist* readers will be more thoughtful contributors. "Leave no answer unquestioned" points to the extra insight *The Economist* articles bring to bear. Because the foundation of *The Economist*'s campaign is a potent brand idea (in-depth analysis), the ads have durability. *The Economist* ads have a subtle creativity – but, importantly, creativity that is linked to a selling message. And it is a selling message that is designed to resonate with a sophisticated, urban and professional target audience. Advertising relying primarily on a cleverness or humour but devoid of a selling message wears out its welcome much quicker.

Frankie and Louie, the Budweiser lizards, wore out. How many times can you say "whazzup" and still remain interesting? And in neither case is there an apparent selling idea. *The Economist* took a meaningful selling idea (in-depth analysis) and translated it into a simple but interesting campaign. A campaign for the long run.

Campaigns for the long term need a compelling selling message. There was a US campaign where an elderly couple funded their retirement from change their guests dropped in the couch. It was really very funny. You see they invite people over and force them to sit in the couch, which they then jiggle a bit, hoping that change will fall out of guests' pockets and into the cushions. But who was the advertiser? What does it say about the brand?

> Advertising relying primarily on a cleverness or humour but devoid of a selling message wears out its welcome much quicker.

Here was another funny one: ranch veterans on horseback trying to herd hundreds of cats. The ads employed great production values

– close-ups of grizzled cowboys talking about the challenges of rounding up feisty felines. This was an ad for systems consulting provider EDS. How ranch hands herding cats enhanced the brand equity of an information systems consulting firm is not so clear.

Funny is fine if it enhances the brand message. Little Caesar's pizza aired ads intended to be humorous. For example, one ad featured a pizza maker so proud of his extra pepperoni creation, he couldn't bear to sell it to a customer. Another ad showed how Little Caesar's extra big pizza makes even the Grand Canyon look small. These ads focused either on the product itself (lots of cheese, extra pepperoni, unusual sizes and so on) or on great value. For the Little Caesar's ads, the humour tied well to the selling message.

Creative advertising is great. For advertising built for the long run, the advertising needs to be creative in a meaningful way. There needs to be strong linkage between the brand and the selling message. Otherwise, you have entertained your consumer, but have failed to add value to your brand. Absolut Vodka very creatively integrated their bottle into their selling message. Absolut Elegance featured the bottle with a black bow tie. Absolut Perfection showed the bottle with a halo. The Absolut ads were memorable for creativity and for communicating a sense of specialness – and versions of these ads ran for many years.

Is your advertising clearly speaking the fundamental truth about your brand? If humorous, is your advertising still delivering a relevant strategic message? Do your ads reflect a core concept that has longevity? Is your advertising built for the long run?

TRUTH

32

A service brand is a personal brand

Some people draw distinctions between "products" and "services". Products are more tangible and physical – shoes, luggage, computers and beer. Services are usually less tangible – banking, insurance and interior design. This distinction between the two can sometimes be blurry – a restaurant will have both more tangible (menu items) and less tangible (professionalism of waiters) attributes.

Delivering a positive customer experience is not always easy – and is sometimes more challenging for brands that are more typically considered services. Controlling the customer experience for products can be easier because a variety of engineering, manufacturing and quality control resources can be focused on a relatively few number of plants and production sites, ensuring a relatively consistent offering. A customer's experience of the brand is linked closely to the capability of the production process to deliver a finished product in line with expectations.

For services, a customer's experience with, and connection to, the brand is not the result of what happens in the factory. Rather, the experience with the brand is directly tied to interactions with one or two people who represent the brand and deliver the brand's promised value. And there may be thousands of individuals scattered around the country (or world) all with the job of delivering the brand promise to customers.

Regis salons are conveniently located in shopping centres around the US, Canada and Puerto Rico. Regis offers better pricing than higher-end salons and yet still promises fashion-knowledgeable stylists able to work well with its clients' hair. This is a compelling proposition for a certain segment of the market. When someone walks in for a cut, their view of the Regis brand will be based significantly on their interaction with their particular hairstylist and the quality of the cut that the stylist delivers. To this customer, advertising no longer matters. The website no longer

> The experience with the brand is directly tied to interactions with one or two people who represent the brand and deliver the brand's promised value.

matters. How close Regis is to where they live no longer matters. What matters is the service delivery of that one stylist. Customer perceptions of the Regis brand are inextricably linked with the experience delivered by their stylist.

Mark Shale, with shops in Chicago, Dallas, Atlanta, Kansas City and St Louis, is a US clothing retailer carrying brands such as Robert Talbott, Zanella, Canali and Tommy Bahama. One of Mark Shale's top salespeople is a woman who works at their St Louis location. Shelly works hard at establishing good connections with clients and prospective customers. She has a wonderful fashion sense – great for advising men. She is very patient and responsive in working with sometimes-demanding affluent clients. Shelly maintains her customer database and provides sales alerts. She offers wardrobe consulting and, having learned the style preferences of her clients, identifies items that would be particularly attractive to them. Much of this is simply good salesmanship, although Shelly fully engages with providing good value to her clients. She has accumulated a number of loyal clients. For them, Shelly is the Mark Shale brand.

Boa Construction does very high-end construction and renovation projects in the US. Boa Construction has access to the kind of craftsmen, materials and project management systems expected of a high-end contractor. One area, though, that Boa pays close attention to is the character of the labourers who work on its sites. Boa often sends workers into clients' homes for renovation and remodelling projects – a disruptive and sensitive process under any circumstances, even more so given the nature of its clientele. Boa wants its on-site workers to be very courteous and respectful, taking extra care to minimise the inconvenience of their presence. Not all carpenters, electricians and painters have the demeanour to work effectively in that environment. Boa Construction understands that the value of its brand is more than just the quality of its finished product, but rests as well in the way the finished product is delivered. It rests in the personal on-site interactions between its workers and the client.

How does a service brand, particularly one with far-flung locations, ensure the kind of personal brand delivery that leads to success? Hiring and training are certainly important in ensuring excellent delivery of the brand experience. Starbucks provides substantial training for its baristas to ensure both consistent product knowledge and good customer relations. Hire for passion about your brand's mission. When in an Apple Store, you sense that the people working there aren't just interested in some position in retailing; rather, they are there because of their enthusiasm for the brand.

With service brands, front-line staff are the face of the brand.

With service brands, front-line staff are the face of the brand. These are the people charged with delivering the experience of your brand. The perceptions your customers have of your brand will be shaped by the personal interactions that occur. It is important that these vital employees understand and embody the spirit of your brand. A service brand is a personal brand.

33

Is your brand the best
at something?
If so, be satisfied

The brand that establishes itself as outstanding in a certain way is fortunate. Examples abound: Volvo for safety, Apple for creative computing and Brooks Brothers for traditional male style. Brands such as these have established a wonderful reputation in a particular domain.

Management, eager to grow sales, often view such specialisation as limiting. Yet pushing a brand beyond its expertise dilutes its focus. Apple tried to expand its appeal to corporate customers – with little success. Brooks Brothers tried to expand its brand to female clothing – with little success. Volvo has muddled its advertising message with a greater emphasis on stylish appearance. But there were already computers well accepted by corporations and retailers specialising in traditional styles for women, and almost every motor manufacturer strives to build a stylish car.

All too frequently, management takes for granted the halo of being the "best" in a particular area. However, to be considered the best in a category, much must have gone right. R&D must have developed a superior product. Marketing must have clearly communicated the benefits. Sales have probably grown consistently, and typically share leadership is accrued to the "best". On top of this, to be the "best" indicates years of consistency. One does not become the best at something overnight. So, all of these various components, from research to manufacturing to marketing to sales, have been operating in a consistently strong manner for years to develop a company's brand into the "best" in the category.

Pushing a brand beyond its expertise dilutes its focus.

Why then, do executives toss aside the mantle of being the "best" so easily? Because in business, the best is never enough, or so they fear. Who will be better than them next year? Unfortunately, it is that very fear that causes changes to a brand portfolio. It is fear that drives management to leverage a strong existing brand into another category. On top of that, business is not about being satisfied. Business is about growth and capitalising on opportunities. However, that is often contradictory to effective brand building. Brands that are the "best" in a category need to work all the harder to stay focused and not allow a chase for growth to dilute the brand.

Consider Kraft. For years, cheese in the US was spelled K-R-A-F-T. Then an acquisition or two happened, and some product proliferation occurred. Before long, Kraft no longer stood for cheese – it stood for a large food company that made all sorts of food products.

Brands that are the "best" in a category need to work all the harder to stay focused.

Rival Sargento jumped on this shift and started to capture the cheese market share once held so dear by Kraft. With the message that Sargento was all cheese all the time, it took that mantle of "being the best" from Kraft. There is no denying that Kraft is a fabulous company. With acquisitions and growth come some difficult decisions. In this case, Kraft wasn't satisfied with being the best at cheese, and that opened the door for other brands to take that mantle.

Jaguar came to represent elite British elegance. To compete in more segments of the market, Ford acquired Jaguar in 1989. To its credit, Ford did much to improve on the spotty reliability record of Jaguar. But corporate pressures to boost sales of Jaguars led to some questionable model decisions. The X-Type was developed as a low-cost entry car. Considered by *Time* magazine to be one of the 50 worst cars of all time, the X-Type was viewed as little more than a spruced up Ford – and then came the station wagon version! Ford was unwilling or unable to let Jaguar be the best at what it could be – a stylishly elegant British driving experience.

David Yurman is a jewellery designer who has captured the hearts of many women. Known for truly distinctive designs, Yurman is a favourite of the very well-heeled American woman. What Yurman has not done is to develop a line of clothing or perfume for this same target. Yurman understands what he is best at – designing jewellery – and has stayed focused on that. This is not to say that the company hasn't seen strong growth, for it has. However, that growth has come by continuing to hone its designing skills and not by moving into new market segments. The more focused Yurman is on design, the more intriguing the products are, the more that well-heeled woman will buy and the greater the growth for the organisation. Being the best is not something this firm takes lightly.

Michael Jordan, arguably the best basketball player in history, returned from a short career in minor league baseball to...well, play basketball again! Don't take a brand that is the best at something and send it off to compete in another sport...it will languish in the minors.

Use your company's limited resources to continue to improve the brand to compete where it is already the best – make your car even safer, make your computer even better for creativity, continue to reinforce traditional male style. Be the best at cheese; develop the ultimate jewellery designs. Don't be too quick to toss the mantle of "the best" aside. Be the best at one thing...and be satisfied. What can your brand be the best at? Knowing this is the first step.

TRUTH

34

Great positionings are enduring

The positioning of your brand is one of your most important branding decisions. The positioning is the primary association built around your brand. If consumers know nothing else about the brand, you hope they will know the brand's central meaning. The brand positioning communicates the brand's point of difference and is a primary way of connecting the brand with its target audience. A good brand positioning is built through consistent communications. A good brand positioning is enduring.

Apple introduced its Macintosh personal computer in the mid 1980s. Billed as "the computer for the rest of us", the Mac heralded an era of easy-to-use computing. The Mac's graphical interface brought intuitiveness to computing. This basic notion – "Macs are easy to use" – has been a fundamental mainstay of a brand now moving into its third decade. Early in the brand's history, Apple ran a commercial featuring two business people poring over DOS manuals, trying for hours

> **A good brand positioning is built through consistent communications.**

to get their computer running. Finally, a third co-worker suggests that maybe they should just get a Macintosh. Apple also has run a campaign featuring two men – one who personifies Windows and the other Apple. The two playfully banter back and forth – the underlying message in each of the ads is Apple computers' ease of use.

Allstate Insurance was founded in 1931. In 1950, it introduced the slogan, "You're in good hands with Allstate." Sometimes shortened to "You're in good hands", this tagline creates a feeling of comfort and confidence – highly relevant associations for an insurance company. Allstate found a positioning around comfort and confidence that has endured for half a century in the US.

In business since 1910, Hallmark has tied its brand closely to the emotion around sharing warm feelings through greeting cards. The association between Hallmark and the emotion of caring was reflected in the tagline, "When you care enough to send the very best." This line was first penned in 1944 and served Hallmark well for many years.

Jack Daniels has created magic around its brand through its homespun, nostalgic association with Lynchburg, Tennessee. Brand advertising and the website use black-and-white photography and old-fashioned typefaces to reinforce the brand's link back to an earlier time. When connecting the brand with its birthplace, Lynchburg, Tennessee, Jack Daniels adds "population 461" to again reinforce its small-town, rural roots. One ad featured the headline, "The same since the '60s. That would be the 1860s." Jack Daniels' positioning has been enduring (and endearing).

Wheaties cereal is over 80 years old. In 1933, the brand began its link with sports through sponsorship of minor league baseball broadcasts and baseball ground advertising. The brand's sponsorship of these broadcasts grew rapidly as Wheaties supported more teams, extending its reach across the US. This tie to sports was embodied in the Wheaties tagline, "Breakfast of Champions," and the brand added testimonials from such baseball legends as Babe Ruth and Jackie Robinson.

In the fifties (that would be the 1950s), consumer research led the company to move away from its sports positioning and focus the brand on kids – certainly children were prime consumers of cereal. The brand teamed up with the Lone Ranger and the Mickey Mouse Club, natural alliances for a brand with this new target. However, this strategic decision was a blunder for the brand (don't let testing override judgement!), with sales at one point dropping 10% in a year. In 1958, Wheaties revisited its strategy and returned to the positioning that had built the brand. Wheaties continues to reinforce this sports/fitness positioning.

Great positionings have longevity. But, the brand must deliver on the positioning for the positioning to be credible. Apple has to continue to ensure that its computers are easy to use. Wheaties needs to maintain the good nutritional value of its cereal. Allstate must guarantee that its customers are, in fact, in good hands should misfortune arrive.

The brand must deliver on the positioning for the positioning to be credible.

The positioning should have longevity, but the brand's tagline can change. With the preceding examples, it is the brand concept (Apple and easy to use, Hallmark and warmth of sharing emotion, Allstate and comfort/confidence, Jack Daniels and rural nostalgia, Wheaties and sports/fitness) that is the positioning. The slogan or tagline is the creative reflection of the positioning. The tagline may evolve to stay contemporary and relevant while the brand concept, the positioning, endures.

What is your brand's positioning? Do you have the discipline to stay true to that positioning over decades?

TRUTH

35

Effective branding begins with the name

"Close-Up", "Kwik Fit", "Bishop's Tipple", "The Body Shop", "Dove" and "Pedigree Chum" – all are great names that reflect the essence of the product or service. Close-Up captures the benefit of a sex-appeal toothpaste. Kwik Fit wonderfully says "quick tyre change". Bishop's Tipple vividly portrays a heritage for a real ale. The Body Shop states simply the nature of the business. Dove brings a gentle image to a soap. Pedigree Chum clearly identifies the niche for which the brand was designed.

Good branding starts with the name – the representation of the brand, conjuring images, concepts and experiences. The name is the foundation for these perceptions. Foundations for buildings can be purely functional or can actually enhance the aesthetics of the structure. Poured cement gets the job done; natural stone also beautifies the building.

And so it is with brand names. A brand name can be purely functional: Pricewaterhouse Coopers, Levi's, Xbox 360, Heinz and Avis. Or the name itself can serve to enhance the perception of the brand. Brands such as PlayStation 3, Showtime and Pret à Manger lay an immediate foundation and create a perception that other marketing activity can enhance. The name itself creates that very first perception.

Despite the obvious value of a good name, a quick tour through the local phone directory shows a number of businesses using meaningless initials: CSR (temping services), FTS (delivery service) and LGT (cabinet work). Or, in a fight to appear in the front of the book, some use a variation of "a" at the start of their name: Aaabco (clearing drains) and about 35 businesses called AAA or A-A (including a car parts shop, a CV writing service, a taxi firm, a key and lock service, a plumbing business and a travel agency). Really, how silly.

The name itself creates that very first perception.

And then there is a local business called Just Wooden Fences. Pretty clear, huh?

In global marketing, a common approach is to "Think Global, Act Local". The spirit of that statement is to bring the brand and the marketing strategies to a region, but to implement those strategies given local influences. When all is said and done, however, a brand may be left with only its name as a global constant.

The packaging may change; different size or formats may be prominent in a country. Colours may have different meanings, so the packaging or even logo may have to be modified.

Even the product itself may change to reflect the global needs. Coca-Cola uses a modified formula in Asia. Asian populations don't appreciate the level of sweetness that western buyers do, so Coca-Cola changes the product formulation to meet those consumer needs. The main constant for Coca-Cola is the brand name.

Maintaining the global name is not easy. The name may have various meanings in different countries. The English version may be difficult to translate or hard for a culture to pronounce. It becomes too easy to buy in to local arguments that a different name for a country or region is needed.

However, if building a global brand is important, the one piece that must remain constant is the name. The name is the foundation for your global brand. In the face of many local activities, stay true to your constant – stay true to your name.

Mergers create their own naming challenges. There is the Fifth Third bank. Any guess how it got its name? The Third Bank merged with the Fifth Bank. Pretty clever, huh? There are now FedEx Kinko's copy centres. Perhaps FedEx would have been better just leaving the Kinko's name (well known for copy centres) separate from the FedEx name (well known for overnight package delivery). The telecom industry has experienced a variety of mergers; one of the largest was SBC and AT&T. After what was certainly much deliberation, the SBC name was dropped in favour of the AT&T brand. This decision was in part due to the broader awareness and international scope of the AT&T brand.

The brand name is the mental hook upon which equities and associations are hung. Naming experts often suggest that a brand name should be short, memorable and unique. Yes, but consider that the name itself should embody the essence of your brand. Consider that the name alone should provide an understanding of what the brand represents or at whom the brand is aimed. You never have to

The brand name is the mental hook upon which equities and associations are hung.

see an advertisement for Brawny paper towels to understand that they are tough. You don't need a brochure to explain the key benefit of Fit N Trim dog food.

Certainly there are many great brands – Apple, McDonald's, Mercedes-Benz, Rolex and Tide – that have no inherent meaning. The meaning and value of these brands have been built through years of advertising and exposure. A name with inherent meaning is not a requirement for creating a successful brand, but it does make the job much easier.

TRUTH

36

Your brand makes your
company powerful,
not the other way around

Companies are always interested in being the leader – in being a powerful voice in the market. Many times, companies believe the "power" is derived from its leadership and that ultimately it is the company that makes the brands powerful. Actually, that can't be further from the truth. Consumers typically don't buy companies, unless they are investing in the stock market. Consumers buy brands. Corporate revenues come from brands. Corporate profits come from brands. It is brands that make a company powerful, not the other way around.

Let's imagine a trip to the Porsche car company. What would you see? You would see some manufacturing facilities – people working on

Corporate profits come from brands.

assembling cars, some automated equipment and cars in various states of finished production. You would see some office areas: finance managers shifting funds among asset classes; accountants reconciling end-of-month figures; marketing people reviewing copy for an upcoming brochure; engineers revising prototypes for a model revision. In fact, you would see pretty much the same activity you would see at any other company.

There is nothing that you would necessarily see or count or catalogue that would capture the value of the Porsche brand. Other companies with less-powerful brand names, such as Kia, have people doing the exact same activities. What makes Porsche as a company powerful is the Porsche brand – a brand built upon years of focused excellence in the domain of sports cars. Engineering a strong heritage of racing tradition that, in turn, carries through to high-performance street cars. Creating exclusivity in the market by building fewer cars, with great care.

The Porsche car company has assets – buildings, equipment, employees and so on. These assets have value in the design, development, manufacturing and selling of cars. If the Porsche company were to liquidate, its employees would find jobs elsewhere, equipment could be sold (at a great discount) and building space could be sold or leased. But the most valuable asset would be the right to the Porsche name and crest.

All too often, companies don't appreciate the power of their brands. Unfortunately, corporate arrogance of power and success frequently gets in the way of potentially successful brands. There is such a strong belief that the power comes from the organisation, that the brands are not carefully managed and supported. When business decline occurs, the corporation doesn't understand why. If the corporation is so powerful, shouldn't consumers be knocking at the door?

Corporate arrogance of power and success frequently gets in the way of potentially successful brands.

One company that got quite caught in this trap was Mennen. Commercials for its products always ended with "By Mennen". There was a belief that the corporation would add power to the brands and thus the tagline. But the brands were lacklustre, and no amount of corporate endorsement could correct that situation.

What is unfortunate is that Mennen used to have some very strong brands. Do you remember Old Spice? How about Speed Stick? Somehow or another, Mennen lost its way. Instead of focusing on the strength of its brands, they thought its corporate "power" could drive the brands instead. Years later, it is now trying to revitalise some of its brands that used to have some market strength.

What about Disney? Disney is a powerful company. See, a company can drive powerful brands, right? Wrong. Let's take a close look at this. Is Disney the company driving the power of the brands? Or are the brands driving the value of Disney? Think of the brands that Disney owns: Shrek and Cinderella, and Goofy and Winnie the Pooh, to name just a few. Each of those brands is a powerhouse in and of itself. When a three-year-old goes to nursery each morning, she doesn't search for her favourite Disney toy – she would not know to ask for Disney. She always looks for Winnie the Pooh. She knows Pooh by name and she loves Pooh.

Her sister is four and loves films. Yes, adults know she loves Disney movies. However, this little one will tell you she loves *The Jungle*

Book and *101 Dalmatians* and *Lady and the Tramp*. There is no denying that Disney is a magical company. It has learned how to harness the energy and power of each of its individual brands to create an enormous business. But, the business of Disney is much like the business of Porsche. There are assets to manage, copy to write and month-end reports to run. It is not the power of Disney that creates the magic of the brands. Pooh and Donald Duck and Snow White are the powerhouse brands that drive the business of Disney – because it is the brand that makes the company powerful.

TRUTH

37

Be consistent but not
complacent

Friends in our lives usually have predictable personalities. There is the clowning-around friend, the shy friend, the ambitious career-driven friend and the sensitive and caring friend. Although our friends have many sides, we experience them in predictable ways. If the shy friend suddenly starts clowning around and being very outgoing, this is a bit unusual.

Brands are like friends. You know them in predictable ways. You expect consistency. You expect them to be true to how you know them. Sometimes the market doesn't accept a brand acting beyond how people have come to know it.

Volkswagen is a very familiar brand – the original Beetle was a quirky, endearing little charmer of a car. Volkswagen has certainly grown up over the years – and the original Beetle is motoring history. However, Volkswagen has worked very hard to connect with a young, hip audience. The Golf, Jetta and new Beetle have been instrumental in reviving the company and helping differentiate Volkswagen from its more stodgy rivals.

> Sometimes the market doesn't accept a brand acting beyond how people have come to know it.

All of this makes its entry into the high-end luxury segment with the Phaeton very puzzling. The Phaeton is no doubt a great car – but it just isn't how people have known their friend Volkswagen. Predictably, the Phaeton has been a sales disaster in the US, since this $60,000–100,000 über-luxury car doesn't fit the VW image. Volkswagen is a perfectly good brand – it just wasn't staying true to how people know it.

Consistency of message is also important. Repetition and consistency is important to implant the brand's meaning in the mind of the target customer – over and over. Think of Levi's and blue jeans, Saturn and friendly car-buying, and Hefty and tough trash bags. Brands that regularly change their message are like people who constantly introduce themselves as something else. First it's, "Hello, I'm Steve. I'm a lawyer." Then it's, "Hi, I'm Steve. I'm a veterinarian." Later, "Hi, I'm Steve. I'm an electrician." Steve will have us so confused, we won't know what he is.

Marketing managers want to believe in the value of consistency, but often argue that they can't keep their brand consistent. The environment is constantly changing and our competitors are changing – the only constant is change, they will say. But do not confuse consistency (a good thing) with *complacency* (a bad thing).

Repetition and consistency is important to implant the brand's meaning in the mind of the target customer.

The first model year for the Porsche 911 was 1963. Across four and a half decades of 911s, the brand has maintained amazing visual consistency. There is a design aesthetic – a fundamental essence to which Porsche has stayed true. Porsche has also stayed true to the 911's basic mission of providing the ultimate sports car experience.

As consistent as Porsche has been with the 911, it has not been complacent. Close examination of 45 years of 911s would reveal the cars to be different from a mechanical and engineering standpoint. Porsche would not be successful trying to sell today 1960s automotive technology. The 1963 911 had a 2.0 litre engine generating 130 horsepower with a 0–60 mph time of 9.0 seconds and a top speed of 130 miles per hour. The most recent 911 Turbo sports a 3.6 litre power plant churning out 480 horsepower, reaching 60 mph in 3.9 seconds and a top speed of 189 miles per hour. Although the 911 has been consistent, it certainly hasn't been complacent.

Breitling is a Swiss watch manufacturer. For decades, Breitling has built its brand image around aviation. It has stayed true to this core message year after year. Its watches, though, are continuously upgraded and updated to stay technologically relevant. A recent addition was a model that contains an emergency locator transmitter. When activated, it transmits your position on an emergency frequency monitored worldwide. This technological advance is perfectly consistent with Breitling's image, because it's a device (automatically activated in case of a crash) universally placed in every aircraft, from a small two-seat Cessna to large jets. Consistency without complacency.

The key to consistency is focus. Without focus, there is nothing to be consistent around. Gap has been struggling because it's losing its focus. Known for comfortable casual basics for younger people, it has tinkered with its merchandise to broaden its appeal. But the newer clothing styles and colours aren't popular. Gap has drifted from how people knew it. Timberland, by contrast, stays consistent without being complacent. Timberland sells clothing and footwear; it freshens its inventory every season. Timberland naturally wants to ensure that its offerings are attractive to its target audience. It isn't complacent. But it is consistent in ensuring that its range reflects a brand oriented towards the outdoors. It ensures that its styles have a certain rugged authenticity about them. Consistency without complacency.

TRUTH

38

Is your brand different?
If not, why will someone
buy it?

A brand has a special meaning when it is unique. By being unique, a brand is differentiated from others and is, therefore, more memorable. Consumers use the brand to assist them in distinguishing products and services. As such, if your brand does not communicate the difference you provide, the consumer will see little reason other than price to purchase it.

Many marketers tend to look at competitors and try to mimic the success a competitor has. When a brand is not differentiated, it does not own a unique position in the consumer's mind. As such, it becomes difficult for a copy cat brand to earn the respect and a sale from the consumer.

It is not just copying a competitor that leads to lack of differentiation. Not clearly understanding the benefits that make your brand a better choice also leads to problems. Clear differentiation is a primary reason that consumers choose a brand.

US retailer Sears has long struggled with this issue. Sales have suffered because consumers have been unable to determine why they should shop at Sears. Sears was, for many years, heralded as the company to go to for just about

> Clear differentiation is a primary reason that consumers choose a brand.

everything. However, with the proliferation of mass merchandisers, combined with the increased popularity of speciality stores, the capability to carry a number of products was no longer unique. Sears could not explain to consumers why it was different, or why they should buy at Sears. So many consumers didn't.

The world is filled with brands that have died because they were not different enough, not unique enough. Izod, 7-Up and IBM personal computers are all brands that, over time, gave the consumer no reason to purchase them. Hush Puppies is a shoe brand that fell into the nondifferentiated abyss in the US. It made products for everyone – men, women and children alike. It tried to claim a bit of comfort, but that was no different from any other shoe brand out there. There was no unique design. There was no flashy ornamentation. On the whole, it wasn't "special"; they were not differentiated shoes. As such, its stateside sales were lacklustre.

For the many failures, there is an equal number of success stories. Enterprise Rent-a-Car understands why it is unique. Whereas all other rental car companies base their business in airports, Enterprise scatters its locations through the community; focusing on customer service..."we pick you up". Consumers understand this uniqueness, see value in this and have recognised it by renting from them.

An interesting category to consider is that of bottled water. The marketers try desperately to differentiate their bottled water from other bottled waters. Importantly, they also differentiate their bottled water from tap water. Consider Fiji Water, which is bottled at the Fiji Islands and is full of minerals. Compare that with Evian, which is natural spring water from the French Alps. The list goes on, and for each type of bottled water, there are small points of difference that are being made. Each seeks a relevant distinction to generate long-term sales and profits.

The video game machine market has been highly competitive, with Nintendo, Microsoft and Sony jostling for the affections of gamers. Sony has been highly successful with its PlayStation franchise (PlayStation, PlayStation 2 and PlayStation 3). Microsoft has put a lot of resources into its Xbox 360. Technological advances have led to increasingly involved and realistic gaming experiences. But those advances also brought games that were complicated for casual gamers to master. Nintendo's Wii became a big hit by moving in the opposite direction. Nintendo developed a simple, intuitive controller and easy-to-play games that attracted legions of consumers who would not normally be interested in video games. Nintendo differentiated its Wii in a way that was highly appealing to an audience not well-served by Sony or Microsoft.

Have you ever walked with a child past a display of sweets? Talk about differentiation! Any four- or five-year-old can clearly explain to you why they love a Picnic but not Snickers. Why Cadbury's Buttons are always their choice over Haribo. The benefits of a Flake over a Kit-Kat. There is no denying that these are all chocolate products. But the industry is famous for creating a unique difference in each of its brands, making that product special for its consumers, and seeing consistent growth as a result.

What is the one, salient point that makes your brand unique?

Identifying a point of differentiation is fundamental to building a brand, but it is difficult. Resist the urge to copy your competitor. Instead, look for opportunities to be unique. What is the one, salient point that makes your brand unique? Can any of your competitors try to claim this point? Are you communicating this difference to your consumers? If your brand does not stand for something special, why should someone buy it?

39

The three Ms of taglines: meaningful, motivating and memorable

Great taglines instantly create meaning around a brand. Pepsi's "Generation Next", Michelin's "Because so much is riding on your tyres" and MasterCard's "Priceless" all nicely capture something special about those brands – Pepsi's association with youth, Michelin's emphasis on safety and trust, and MasterCard's connection to our day-to-day lives.

Powerful taglines should embody three characteristics. They should be *meaningful*, *motivating* and *memorable*. Let's take these three Ms and consider them individually from the consumer's perspective. A tagline must be meaningful. What is meaningful about the brand to the target audience? Why should your target care? If it is not meaningful, why will consumers buy it?

Powerful taglines should embody three characteristics.

A good example of a meaningful brand tagline was for the brand Sega. Sega used "Welcome to the next level" as its tagline for its video game system. This reference, referring to every gamer's goal of getting to the next level within a game, connected well with the younger audience Sega targeted.

Meaningful messages often deliver in two ways: something about the consumer and something about the brand. Sega is a good example that this can be effectively done. "Welcome to the next level" speaks, of course, to the gamer's individual goal for himself or herself. The tagline also speaks to the superiority of Sega games and the increased challenge at each level. With both a personal message and product message at work, the meaningfulness of the brand's tagline is greatly enhanced.

Meaningful messages often deliver in two ways: something about the consumer and something about the brand.

Consider, too, the idea of motivating. It is not enough to have a meaningful tagline – it must motivate as well. The essence of motivating is to cause the target audience to want to purchase. The tagline needs to help stimulate the target audience to take action. To take action with a product, frequently a tagline will stimulate action in a person's life as well.

Does the tagline motivate your target to see the brand as important and, ultimately, include the brand as part of their life? Apple has been successful in creating a line of products that is significantly differentiated from its competitors. Apple's tagline "Think Different" is simultaneously a statement of its corporate philosophy and a motivational rally point for legions of Apple fans who see themselves as willing to be different.

Finally, think about memorable. If a tagline is meaningful and motivating, but no one remembers it, will it drive sales? Most likely, no. A tagline needs to stay with an audience. It needs to be in their frame of reference when it is time to make that purchase, when a need must be answered.

Clever taglines can certainly be memorable. Energizer's "It keeps going and going and going..." is an example of where cleverness captures the imagination of customers. However, sheer force of repetition can etch a simple phrase indelibly in consumers' minds as well. Maxwell House's "Good to the last drop" and BMW's "The ultimate driving machine" are both testimony to the power derived from the consistent use of the same line year after year.

Nike has longed used its "Just Do It" tagline. Nike embodies the essence of the three Ms in this tagline, which is why it is now such a ubiquitous line – understood, accepted and loved by so many worldwide. The concept of "Just Do It" is meaningful. It is meaningful in terms of the product, and it is meaningful to the lives of the target that Nike is trying to reach.

The tagline "Just Do It" is motivating as well. People take it as an individual challenge to perform. It also motivates purchase, of course. Buying the product will help the consumer meet personal challenges. It is so motivating, that a friend was mentioning that her eight-year-old son firmly believes he will jump better in basketball with Nike shoes on. He believes he can perform better and have an advantage over his friends, because of the Nike promise.

Of course, it is exceptionally memorable. It is so powerful, that Nike can go to just the "swish" logo and consumers immediately translate that to "Just Do It". They don't need to see or hear the words to get the message.

Spend time honing this important tool – keep it meaningful, motivating and memorable.

Although many factors contribute to a brand's success, the tagline has great potential for enhancing the brand's meaning. As you build your brand, consider the three Ms. Is your tagline delivering your brand message in a way that is meaningful, motivating and memorable?

TRUTH

40

Customer service is the touch point of your brand

Improving customer service is not the most glamorous of marketing tasks. Advertising can be great fun. Travelling with the sales force can be enlightening. But the nuts and bolts of focusing on customer service can be an important component of your brand's success.

Customer service vividly reflects your brand. It is your brand promise brought to life in a one-on-one interaction. Product return hassles, long delays "on hold", transfers from person to person, careless delivery people and grouchy people at the counter all help to sour feelings towards a brand. Often these interactions come just as your customer is making a purchase (placing a phone order, paying at the till) or trying to repair a problem (product return). These interactions are sometimes the last contact with your brand before the long delay until the next purchase.

Many people often complain about automated phone services. You call in to change your cable or your phone provider and you are responding to a recorded voice.

Customer service vividly reflects your brand.

For the cable or phone companies, these automated systems are a cost-effective way to walk customers through many common issues and questions. Unrecognised, however, is the brand cost of losing a powerful opportunity to engage with a consumer and create a positive experience about the brand.

Enterprise car rental understands the importance of the one-on-one time with its customers. Pop into an Enterprise office and you will be cheerily greeted by well-groomed, well-dressed young men and women. (Enterprise is the biggest recruiter of fresh college graduates in the US.) Your questions and requests will be handled politely and efficiently. You are left feeling good about your choice to use Enterprise and feeling good towards the brand.

Enterprise starts all its employees on the "shop floor" – washing cars, greeting customers and processing rental agreements. Starting out washing cars isn't really about training its employees to be better car washers. Rather, it instils early on some humility and understanding of the importance of serving the customer. Enterprise fully appreciates customer service as the touch point with its brand.

Many western computer companies have been shifting their call centres overseas. In the spirit of offering a live and hopefully positive brand experience, they are looking for the middle road between automated systems and a costly local customer service system. The personal one-on-one experience with the brand can powerfully drive the brand message. That is, until one finds someone on the customer service side who is not a fluent English speaker. A potentially positive brand touch point can change very quickly. Not only is the customer service person not easily understood, but also the problem may not be resolved as quickly.

For many companies, customer service is considered an expense. Frequently seen as part of operations, the focus is on how effectively and efficiently questions, claims or issues are resolved. However, customer service is a clear opportunity to create a strong one-on-one brand experience with each customer. When customer service is considered as part of the overall brand experience, it puts this critical function into an entirely different light.

Lands' End is a well-known brand. Its service is uniquely delivered through its customer operations. You may receive a catalogue or you may choose to order online. Frequently however, customers prefer to call in. Why not? Very knowledgeable, well-trained operators can work with you on any of your various questions, from materials used, to sizing to colour options. And they are friendly! Lands' End has unlocked the secret to customer service. The customer service touch point for Lands' End is truly a centrepiece of the brand experience.

Customer service is a critical component in brand building. The touch point provided by customer

> Customer service is a clear opportunity to create a strong one-on-one brand experience.

service is a unique opportunity to create a one-on-one experience between each of your customers and your brand. Customer service is a powerful tool to have in your arsenal of brand-building activities. Customer service may not have the glamour of an advertising shoot in Tokyo. However, it does have a truly unique capability to build strong brand experiences and ultimately brand preference, one person at a time.

TRUTH

41

Smaller targets are easier to hit

An archery club was practising. All lined up, each person faced what seemed to be a small target hung in front of a bale of hay. Perhaps if those targets were larger, they would have a better chance of success? On the archery range, a nice big target can be easy to hit.

In marketing, however, the opposite is true. Large targets are difficult to hit. The more diverse group you hope to appeal to, the harder it is to construct a compelling brand proposition, and the tougher it is to build meaning around your brand that connects with your potential customers.

A Washington bookshop, Politics and Prose, has built a wonderful business focused around the intellectual community, stocking thoughtful poetry, policy analysis books and other provocative works that engage the reader in contemporary issues. Foregoing the temptation to broaden the store's appeal, staying focused actually makes it easier for Politics and Prose to resonate with its customers. Carefully defining the target audience helps it select its inventory, special events and speakers, and communications. Such clarity enhances the shop's distinctiveness.

Politics and Prose is a great example of a small business that has thrived amid changing business dynamics – the growing popularity of large booksellers such as Barnes & Noble and Borders, as well as internet competitors such as Amazon.com. Developing a meaningful niche and building a business around a specific customer segment helps isolate Politics and Prose from formidable competitors.

Creating a brand's bull's-eye is the role of a target audience description. A target audience description details a brand's *most likely* prospect. Developing a rich, thorough target audience description underpins effective marketing and brand building. Understanding your target audience, and appreciating what gives their lives meaning, leads to a message about your brand that connects with their reality. Such a description provides an aiming point.

Don't be reluctant to depict precisely the kind of person at whom the brand is aimed. The question "Who is your target?" is sometimes answered with "Well, pretty much everyone". Although it may be true that everyone could possibly afford, use and get value from a brand, some people simply make better prospects than others. A person may be a better prospect because of their values, their life stage, where they live and so on. What brand message could possibly bring meaning to "Well, pretty much everyone"?

Creating a brand's bull's-eye is the role of a target audience description.

More common than "Well, pretty much everyone" is a target that is still simply too broad. Consider the over-used target "female shoppers, age 25–54". Including "shoppers" adds nothing insomuch as every female (and male) is a "shopper" at one time or another. Here are two females, age 25–54. The first, a single 27-year-old college dropout, has three children and lives in rural Suffolk. Living with her mother, her full-time job, bringing £12,000 a year, helps with shared expenses. The second, a married 45-year-old graduate, lives in Glasgow. Their household income totals £120,000. They have a part-time nanny helping with their two children.

So, there are two "female shoppers, age 25–54". To which one are you directing your brand's message? Without knowing the answer to that question, a meaningful message can't possibly be crafted. Your message is meaningful when it is motivating and relevant to your audience. You can't know your message until you know your audience.

A good target audience description should include demographics, geography and psychographics. Demographics include characteristics such as age, income, household size, education, gender and marital status. Geography can be scaled up or down as appropriate. A small local business might focus on a particular suburb or part of town. A domestic company might find that its best prospects are on the coast or maybe in the southeast. An international brand may choose to focus on particular countries or parts of the world. Psychographics reflects values, lifestyles and attitudes and enriches the target audience description.

A specific, well-crafted target audience will be a more homogenous group – a group that shares similar motivations and desires. A group that market research can focus on to uncover important triggers for purchase. A group for which a compelling brand message can be crafted.

A few caveats are in order. First, any target audience has to be large enough to support the financial objectives and business model of the brand. The target audience for a soft drink is likely to be larger than the target for an expensive luxury car. Second, having a well-defined, clear target does not mean that others won't be attracted to your brand. There's no gatekeeper refusing to sell to those outside your target audience. Power, though, comes from a deep understanding of the kind of person most likely to be attracted to your brand. And that deep understanding comes from having a focused, detailed target audience description.

A large target might be great on the archery range. But when developing a brand, a much smaller target is preferable. A smaller target is easier to hit.

Power comes from a deep understanding of the kind of person most likely to be attracted to your brand.

TRUTH

42

Beware of the allure of brand extensions

The secret to building a great brand is consistency and focus. However, this can be terribly difficult to do. As soon as a brand does well, companies like to take the brand and extend the name to many other products. In theory, it is understandable. Why spend large sums building a new brand when there is a perfectly fabulous brand sitting there and waiting to be used? By extending the brand, consistency and focus are typically lost. However, what is the long-term cost of neglecting a brand versus the immediate savings from not having to create a new brand? Is it better in the long run to build a brand from scratch or develop a brand extension?

> By extending the brand, consistency and focus are typically lost.

In a cost-focused, corporate environment, the answer is too simple. Extend the brand – take the name of an existing brand into new categories. Hooters starting an airline, Heinz introducing a cleaning vinegar, Reese's bringing to market lip balm, *Cosmopolitan* (the woman's magazine) launching a brand of yogurt – these are just a few wacky examples.

There are two dominant brands of chicken in the US: Perdue and Tyson. Tyson completed a $4.6 billion merger with beef and pork producer IBP. As a result, Tyson owned a number of beef and pork brands that were a part of the IBP empire.

Tyson management had several options. One approach could have been to take the best known of the IBP beef and pork brands and concentrate marketing efforts on building greater consumer awareness and affinity with the stronger brands. Tyson could reinforce its connection with "chicken" and then build separate strong brands for beef, pork and ready-to-cook home meals.

However, Tyson decided to scrap all the IBP brands and instead place the "Tyson" name on beef, pork and other assorted products. Essentially, management created a number of brand extensions – a range of disparate meat products all under the "Tyson" name.

The logic is there. "Tyson" is a well-recognised brand that consumers identify as good quality. But the link is there in customers' minds between "Tyson" and "chicken". Why not build equally strong links between a different brand name and "pork"? The more the "Tyson" name is spread around, the greater the chance of weakening the association between "Tyson" and "chicken" – an outcome rival Perdue would love to take advantage of.

Tyson planned a $40 million dollar advertising campaign behind the tagline, "Tyson. It's what your family deserves." This meaningless slogan could apply equally as well to a bank, a car or a home computer. Tyson management forgot what the Tyson brand really means...and soon possibly so will consumers.

The vigilance required by brand managers is critical when it comes to brand extensions. Before an extension can be considered, brand leaders need to truly understand what their brand stands for in the marketplace. Whereas Tyson clearly stands for chicken for many consumers, BMW stands for the "ultimate driving machine". For BMW, it is about driving performance. Its brand is not limited to cars. It is appropriate for motorcycles as well.

US brand Healthy Choice struggled mightily with its brand extensions. When Healthy Choice was first introduced, it was as frozen dinners. As the consumers hopped up on the healthy bandwagon, brand marketers at Healthy Choice decided to extend the brand into numerous other categories. Before long, there were Healthy Choice biscuits and Healthy Choice crackers, with all sorts of products in between. As Healthy Choice embarked on one brand extension after another, the brand started to falter. In each case, the extension was a product that stood

> Vigilance is critical when it comes to brand extensions.

for a low-fat, healthy option. But the consumer understood the brand to stand for frozen dinners – healthy frozen dinners, but frozen dinners all the same. The consumers struggled to apply the Healthy Choice brand to other food options, handicapping these Healthy Choice brand extensions.

If the position of the brand is not clearly understood, then an inappropriate extension will dilute and confuse the message of the brand. No doubt the allure is there. What a great way to build volume for a brand – extend it a bit. Right? Wrong! Beware the allure of the brand extension; it may provide a short-term financial gain that ultimately erodes your brand.

TRUTH

43

Keep advertising simple,
but not simplistic

The camera holds tight on a Master Lock as a bullet penetrates the lock casing, but the lock holds steadfast. A distinguished gentleman in a tuxedo adds his soiled handkerchief, some ice, some water and All-Temperature Cheer detergent to a Martini mixer, shakes and removes the clean handkerchief. Early VW Beetle advertising used uncluttered visuals of the car with straight-forward headlines such as "$1.02 a pound", "Think small" and "If you run out of gas, it's easy to push". Folksy Tom Bodett pitched Motel 6 as a basic good-value place to stay and promised to "leave the light on for you". Each of these classic US ads had a very clear message delivered with laser-sharp crispness.

People are bombarded by a never-ending stream of commercial messages. How much do they notice? Not a lot. How much do they retain? Even less.

The most effective advertising is simple. Simple in concept. Simple in execution. Simple advertising is understandable. Simple advertising is memorable.

Simplistic implies trite and trivial. Neither is desirable, yet there seems to be no shortage of trite and trivial advertising. There have been the Burger King ads with a large, oversized "king" showing up to tell viewers...what exactly? There have been the funny ads featuring cavemen and Geico insurance. The cavemen were so popular, they even got their own (short-lived) TV show, but what was their message about Geico?

The most effective advertising is simple.

Responsibility for simple advertising rests with both the client and the ad agency. It is the client's responsibility to identify the one main point the ad should deliver about the brand. Yes, one main point. Not two, not three...one. If the client hasn't done this, the agency needs to ask for it. The one main point should be tangible, meaningful and distinctive.

The agency's task is to develop an ad – TV, print, web, radio or outdoor – that clearly communicates that simple idea in a creative and interesting way. Creativity should enhance the communication of one main point – help the communication break through the clutter of competing messages.

Tabasco ran an ad featuring a man sitting on his porch on a hot steamy evening. He is dousing his bread with Tabasco hot sauce. He keeps eating and pouring more Tabasco sauce on his bread. A mosquito lands on his bare leg, takes a bite and flies off. A few seconds later, the mosquito explodes, and we cut to the grinning man. Simple, creative execution delivering the basic message that Tabasco sauce really brings the heat.

In a Philips ad for its long-life light bulbs, a young man sits reading a paper by the light. The light goes out and he replaces the bulb with a Philips long-life bulb, returning to his paper. The light goes out again. As he screws in a new long-life bulb and the light comes back on, the viewer sees he is now an old man – very simple concept, very simple execution.

In the public service domain, an organisation called The Truth has run several very powerful antismoking ads in the US. One ad shows a large van pulling up to the headquarters of a major tobacco company. The people with the van unload 1,200 body bags to depict the number of people who die of tobacco-related illnesses each day. Again, a focused message – simple, direct and creatively delivered.

Be on the lookout for ads that are so creative, they mask the fact that there is no selling idea. Such ads often play to laughs and smiles in the company but do little to influence the intended consumer. Also beware of the ad that stuffs so many selling messages into it, nothing will stand out to the viewer. Both need strategic help. In the first case, the brand team and agency need to find something motivating to focus the brand around. In the second case, fat needs trimming.

For your brand, spend time determining the one main point you want your advertising to communicate (the concept). Ask your agency or creative team to communicate that one main point with focus and impact (the execution). Don't fall in love with fancy art direction or elaborate production values. Don't let creativity hinder clarity. Don't rely on your agency to gloss over your lack of a clear strategy.

Don't let creativity hinder clarity.

Be simple in what you say. Be simple in how you say it.

TRUTH

44

It's a long walk from the
focus group room to the
cash register

Focus groups are ubiquitous – a relatively easy, inexpensive and quick way to take the pulse of the consumer. Brand managers and agency staff lounge in a darkened room, behind a two-way mirror, enjoying soft drinks, finger sandwiches and M&Ms while eight to ten consumers critique their work. Focus groups evaluate product ideas, advertising storyboards, package designs and promotional programmes.

"If you saw this jalapeno-flavoured milk mix at your store, would you be interested in trying it?" asks the moderator.

"Yes, I might try it out," responds one participant.

"It seems interesting," replies another.

"If I had a coupon, I might consider it," adds a third participant.

"It certainly sounds different," a sceptical woman replies.

The marketing manager, eager to launch such a spin-off brand, scribbles notes to herself: "good interest in trying...like that it is different...be sure to include a coupon programme...."

Would you be surprised to find a year later that this jalapeno-flavoured mix was mouldering in the warehouse? This fictitious example may seem a stretch, but many businesses make significant decisions based, in part, on interest shown by consumers in these groups.

In a focus group, people generally want to be helpful. It costs them nothing to say, at least, they find the idea interesting. It costs them nothing to say, yes, they might try it. Lukewarm responses are optimistically interpreted by marketing managers, hopeful that favoured ideas will come to fruition.

Focus groups are an important research tool – when used in conjunction with other research and supplemented by sound management judgement. Focus groups provide great colour commentary. What about: the ad is liked/disliked? What about: the package is confusing? How does this product taste? What do you think about this brand? Do you like this promotion idea? Why? Why not?

But marketing managers often make the mistake of quantifying focus groups. Imagine a focus group discussing five different ad campaign ideas. Carefully listening to the thoughts and reactions to each of the campaign ideas gives a valuable perspective on what is important to consumers, what in each idea is connecting with the participant.

But, inevitably the client wants participants to choose their favourite – fine if such a question then launches fresh discussion for qualitative insight. Tabulating the result, though, has no value. Clients will say, "I know this isn't really meaningful, but let's see how many participants preferred each campaign idea." Even knowing the pointlessness of counting "votes" doesn't prevent people from wanting to do so!

Focus groups are not a bad thing; they can be relatively quick, inexpensive barometers for enhancing management judgement by bringing in the voice of the consumer. Skilful moderators can set participants at ease and navigate smoothly around some of the potential pitfalls of focus groups to ensure a fair exploration of the items on the discussion guide.

Participant comments can contribute to making better branding decisions – maybe revealing something about the ad that hadn't been considered. Sometimes uncovering an insight leads to a product modification. Certainly focus groups help you develop a greater empathy with your target audience, who are often very different from yourself.

What are some ways to maximise value from focus groups? First, don't overload the discussion guide. You don't want the moderator or the participants rushed. One of the key advantages of focus groups is the ability to explore comments in greater depth and engage the participants in dialogue that yields insight. Overloading the discussion guide can inhibit rich exploration.

Don't overload the discussion guide.

Second, take notes but refrain from drawing conclusions prematurely. Listen to ALL the participants. Attend ALL the groups that are held on the topic of interest. Drawing conclusions prematurely will bias your interpretation of the rest of the groups.

Third, resist the temptation to quantify anything. There are research tools and techniques that are well suited for drawing quantitative inferences. A focus group isn't one of them.

Resist the temptation to quantify.

Finally, at the end of the evening's sessions, listen carefully to the moderator's comments and observations. Often the people behind the mirror are eager to talk about what was learned from the groups. This is fine, but listen first to the moderator. The moderator will be the most objective person in the room and can temper overly optimistic (or pessimistic) interpretations of the focus groups.

Focus groups can be an important tool in providing consumer insight into your brand. But when it comes to spending money, it is a long walk from the focus group room to the cash register.

TRUTH

45

Repositioning can be a fool's errand

Marketing managers sometimes talk about "repositioning their brand". Brand managers are expected to have the ability to do this. Many organisations change brand managers frequently, with an expectation that each manager will "reposition" their brand in a way that the previous manager could not. If they reposition often enough, surely at some point they will hit on something. Right? Wrong!

What if brand managers do not completely control or own the brand? A brand resides in a consumer's mind. At best, brand managers can influence its meaning. But in the end, brand management is about creative activities that "cause" a certain "effect" in the marketplace. It is the accumulation of these effects, created in a consumer's mind, that define a brand. So, brand managers don't have full ownership of the brand – the consumer does. Brand managers have responsibility for brand stewardship and try to influence the brand in the minds of the consumer. But, in the end, the consumer will determine whether he or she will accept the marketing influences.

If brand managers don't clearly own the brand, but merely influence it, then how in the world can they possibly reposition it? To reposition means that we need to change what currently exists in a consumer's mind about a brand and shift it significantly enough to take on a new meaning. Although it can be possible to reposition a brand – Lucozade's transformation from a drink to help people recover from illness to a sports drink for athletes is a good example – such transformations are typically expensive and take years to achieve.

So, why is "repositioning a brand" such a common phrase in marketing departments? Typically, this stems from either some change in the environment (a new trend, competitive entry and so on) or simply management's impatience and desire to "make something happen". Such a so-called strategy is either mislabelled or foolish. Let's consider each case.

First up...consider a brand that has not been well managed, carefully defined, or clearly understood. Year after year, the marketing plan changes the focus of the brand. One year, it is a traditional brand for mothers. The next year, the brand group decides a more contemporary image is appropriate. The following year, a new brand team broadens the appeal by including men in the target. And so it goes. Each new brand team declares they are "repositioning

"Repositioning" for a brand that has no positioning doesn't make sense.

the brand". But – and here's the catch – the brand was never clearly positioned to begin with! To say "repositioning" for a brand that has no positioning doesn't make sense.

Consider Kimball Office, a US brand of office furniture. Kimball Office competed with the likes of Herman Miller, Knoll and Hayworth. Its management sought to reposition Kimball Office yet again, so it could compete more effectively with these giants in the industry. What did Kimball Office mean in the marketplace? It stood for pianos and really beautiful hand-crafted wood furniture. But Kimball hadn't made pianos in over 10 years. Most of its business had shifted from high-end wood furniture to metal systems. The brand as the customer understood it had great strength, but it did not have much permission to move into other products. You couldn't simply reposition the brand to be new and contemporary, despite what management wanted. The marketplace wouldn't stand for it. So, according to the consumer, repositioning was not an option.

Brands, like Kimball Office, that are not clearly managed will limp along – never attaining their potential. Marketing managers will come and go – secure in their contribution to the brand's "repositioning". The real tragedy is the second case, an already well-positioned brand.

Building a strong brand requires years of consistent investment. Achieving a solid positioning (Bounty = absorbent, Crest = dental health, easyJet = low cost air travel) is to be cherished, not scrapped. Minds are very difficult to change. Imagine if easyJet decided to reposition the brand as "luxury international air travel". First, it would be throwing away years and millions of pounds in brand-building investment. Second, it will be very, very difficult to think of easyJet as anything but low cost air travel. As a consumer of easyJet, would you ever give it permission to be elegant international air travel?

The first case is so common. Brand positions that fluctuate year to year are challenges many companies struggle with fixing. That still doesn't mean that repositioning is the answer. It means that understanding your brand equities and building consistency to its message is the solution.

The second case of a strongly developed position in the market is to be cherished. Look not to reposition, to destroy the place you own in the consumer's mind. Look instead to build upon the brand's heritage. The point forgotten in repositioning is that brand building occurs over time. So, the investment you made 2 years ago, 5 years ago or 10 years ago all leads to the brand that you own today. Trying to reposition is not just about making a move in this year – it is about undoing the work of all the previous years. In a world that cares about short-term profits, it is easy to lose sight of the total investment made in the brand over the years. However, although companies lose sight of that, the consumer certainly does not.

Build upon the brand's heritage.

Clearly understand your position in the consumer's mind. Identify brand equities to leverage. Be proud of who you are; reinforce the positioning you have. Repositioning can be a fool's errand.

TRUTH

46

With advertising, don't expect too much

Advertising is an important marketing tool. Advertising can communicate a brand's distinction (a roll of Andrex as "soft, strong and very long"), can permeate our social fabric ("Beanz Meanz Heinz", "Because I'm worth it", "Whazzup?") and can raise awareness of important social issues ("THINK! Don't Drink and Drive"). Advertising brings high expectations. It is an expensive and highly visible marketing tool. But it is simply one tool, of many, that contributes to a brand's success.

Advertising brings high expectations.

Volkswagen has had its ups and downs in the US market, having lost $1 billion a year over the past few years. To resurrect sagging fortunes, VW hired the widely acclaimed agency Crispin Porter & Bogusky to revitalise its brand. The agency's new ads featured Helga, a very Teutonic and very sexy blonde. Speaking with a German accent, and clearly targeting young men, Helga highlighted the, ummm, performance features of its GTI model.

Crispin Porter & Bogusky also developed a series of ads themed "safe happens". These ads portrayed very realistic driving scenes, putting the viewer right in the VW. Suddenly, the car is hit. Although the car is damaged, the occupants are fine, and the ads closed with "safe happens".

These ads were well produced. Crispin Porter & Bogusky is a respected agency. But VW was having problems beyond the capability of advertising to solve. VW was perceived as having lower quality than its Japanese rivals and ranked in the bottom 20% for reliability, quality and service according to J.D. Power & Associates. These are serious business issues, requiring brand improvements on many fronts. For VW, advertising can raise front-of-mind awareness. Advertising might encourage car shoppers to drop by a dealership. But it will take more than creative ads to get the brand back on track.

Audi introduced its R8 sports car – a Lamborghini-sourced 420 horsepower mid-engine, four-wheel drive, two-seater beast. To introduce this new model to a wide audience, Audi ran an R8 ad during the Super Bowl. The ad reprised a scene from *The Godfather*. In Audi's ad, a man wakes up to find the chopped-off front-end grill of a luxury car in his bed. Cut to outside of the mansion. The Audi R8 fires up its engine and speeds away as the script "old luxury just got put on notice" appeared on screen.

Launching at the biggest US media event of the year generates awareness – perfect for a new brand like the R8. More than just awareness, though, Audi created an attitude for its new model.

But awareness and attitude alone won't be enough to ensure the success of the R8. Overall image and perceptions of parent company Audi are a factor. The capability to credibly support a model outside Audi's normal market is a factor. The price of the R8 relative to its key competitors will make a difference.

Let's keep going. People's experiences at their local Audi dealership are important. Arrogant or nonresponsive salespeople (yes, there are some) can send potential R8 buyers to Porsche or BMW. Previous experience (good or bad) with Audi cars will shape people's view of the R8. Reviews by magazines such as *What Car?* and *Top Gear* will matter.

Audi has created a dynamic and evolving website in support of the R8. Product brochures at dealerships are an important information resource for potential customers. Audi's involvement with racing will help enhance the R8's image.

Audi's creative and compelling advertising is only one small piece of a large effort to build the R8 brand. Audi understands the importance of advertising but also knows not to expect too much from this one tool.

Hank Seiden, in his book, *Advertising Pure and Simple*, says that all advertising can do is persuade an interested person to try your product once. Seiden certainly helps place expectations for advertising in a perhaps more realistic perspective. Even achieving Seiden's modest goal would be a major accomplishment for advertising. Many of the advertising messages you are exposed to each day simply roll over you unnoticed.

All advertising can do is persuade an interested person to try your product once.

Advertising isn't the end-all in marketing. There are many ways to get a message to a target audience. There are many important tools for building a strong brand.

For many, advertising is an unwanted intrusion, a distraction. Advertising gains some power through consistently delivering the same simple message time after time. Advertising gains some power when the message is delivered with sufficient spending to crack through consumers' indifference. Advertising can work for your brand, but don't expect too much.

TRUTH

47

Don't let testing override judgement

Companies love to test things to death. Why? Probably for several reasons. It seems like the smart, responsible, logical, MBA sort of thing to do. Another common reason is a lack of confidence by marketing managers. Especially when their career began in some area other than marketing, research can serve as a safety net. Also, companies consist of several levels of management. Senior management, not close to lower-level decision making, isn't fond of hearing that the troops in the trenches are making decisions based on intuition.

Nope, they need to generate research and analyses. They need to cautiously pursue the lowest-risk option. They certainly don't want to jeopardise their jobs by shooting from the hip. Research is the ultimate CYA (cover your arse). So the testing machine gets cranked up – focus groups pick apart ideas, surveys uncover "statistically significant differences" and everyone wants to know top-two-box scores. This isn't an indictment of research. Simply consider research as augmenting, not replacing, judgement.

There are many problems in allowing testing to override judgement. To begin with, marketing is sometimes most effective when based on a creative, poignant insight. The science of testing, if relied on extensively, can obscure that

Simply consider research as augmenting judgement.

creative insight. The first principle frequently sacrificed is a focused message. There is no denying that research will show that different consumers will like different things. But, not every item that tests well needs to be included in the advertising.

General Motors implemented a brand management system to guide product development and marketing. Its system has been criticised as producing bland vehicles designed by focus groups. The passion was gone, as models were not created through inspiration, but rather research and testing.

Bob Lutz, brought over from Chrysler, was known as a "car guy", having overseen such innovative models as the Viper, Prowler and PT Cruiser. He disbanded the brand management structure and became personally involved in the design process. Lutz knows the importance of not letting testing override judgement.

Marketing is sometimes most effective when based on a creative, poignant insight.

Design- and science/technology-based companies particularly struggle with the concept of marketing testing. For a scientifically oriented company, the products it makes are heavily researched. It is testing, not judgement, that will get a new food ingredient approved by the regulators. So, in these environments, research is expected to provide the answers. However, in marketing new ideas, new concepts can seem strange at first to consumers comfortable with the familiar. Consumers may react negatively to something simply because it is very different to them. Solely relying on research will never let those intriguing ideas reach fruition, as they usually require managerial judgement to take a step outside the safety net. For the research-oriented organisation, this is a very uncomfortable move – an uncomfortable move made even more so because judgement might not be supported by that which is held so dear: research.

In design industries, striking the appropriate balance between research and judgement can also be challenging. A creative solution, by its very nature, is different from what currently exists. Consumers may not immediately respond favourably. Kimball Office furniture constantly researches its new furniture concepts. Unfortunately, when a particular element of the design did not test well with consumers, it was all too easy to remove that element of the desk or chair from the overall design. As a result, the design industry would frequently say that although Kimball made great furniture, it was always missing the little details that would make the furniture absolutely fabulous. Perhaps a little bit more reliance on creative judgement and less reliance on research results could take the Kimball range from great to fabulous.

Research has a very strong place in marketing. It provides important insights on which to make solid decisions. However, research in and of itself cannot substitute for judgement. With marketing expertise, supported by research insights, judgement can allow the passion of the brand to emerge and capture the attention of the market it serves.

TRUTH

48

Effective advertising is 90% what you say, 10% how you say it

Tremendous energy goes into developing interesting advertising. Writers, art directors, producers, TV directors, editing houses and music studios converge to produce 30 seconds of video. Sometimes the result is groundbreaking work, such as Apple's "1984" spot introducing the Macintosh. (The lone female runner hurls her hammer towards the large screen depicting Big Brother.) Sometimes it's a misguided missile like Coca-Cola's widely criticised US campaign, which depicted nice moments (such as graduation) degenerating into an ugly fight over Coke.

All this activity (lighting sets, casting calls, scouting locations and storyboarding) centres around the "how to say it" element of advertising. Although how you say it (the execution) is important, far more important is what you say (the strategy). A powerful, meaningful message can overcome a bland execution. But an exciting, vibrant execution does not compensate for the lack of a brand story.

Print advertising in the US for Viagra featured various men candidly discussing how Viagra has improved the quality of their romantic relationships and urging the reader to speak to a doctor. There was nothing particularly dramatic about these ads. There weren't unusual fonts, clever headlines or eye-grabbing graphics – nothing that was particularly "creative". There was simply straight talk around a compelling and important message. This campaign's success resided not in a creative execution, but rather in the brand message.

> An exciting, vibrant execution does not compensate for the lack of a brand story.

Apple's recent TV campaign had two guys standing against a sparse white background. One of the guys represented Apple, and the other guy PC. The Apple guy was dressed in a casual style, whereas the PC guy was in a business suit. They simply talked back and forth. Their conversation, though, highlighted key differences between a Mac and a PC – ease of connectivity, built-in features and simplicity of use. The advertising was creative in bringing to life the Mac and PC personas. But what made the advertising *effective* was the way it communicated the compelling and meaningful differentiation of Apple.

Who is responsible for the "what you say", and who is responsible for the "how you say it"? The marketing/brand team must ensure that there is a relevant message for the brand, a point of difference that will resonate with the target audience. Although the brand's ad agency can participate in identifying this relevant difference, it is fundamentally the responsibility of the company to ensure that its products and services have found a purposeful niche in the market. Without this relevant difference, there is no starting point for the agency.

The ad agency is primarily responsible for the "how you say it". It is the agency's job to turn the "what you say" into an interesting, creative execution. But without the meaningful message, the agency will not have anything to direct its creative energy towards. The result may be advertising that is clever and funny but without purpose. This type of advertising can be dangerous since it creates the *appearance* of good advertising but lacks the necessary substance.

The Mini Cooper has focused on developing its brand around a "fun small car". Its US agency, Crispin Porter & Bogusky, brought this message to life in a variety of creative ways. There was the "mini" product brochure on the Mini. There was the Encyclopedia of Open Motoring, highlighting the fun and the virtues of top-down travel in the Mini convertible. There were numerous ads that had fun with the small size of the Mini Cooper. The work for Mini Cooper led to a number of advertising industry awards for Crispin Porter & Bogusky. That's the "how you say it". But the business success of Mini Cooper rests to a larger degree in the strategic niche the brand developed. That's the "what you say".

A recent US campaign that seemed heavy on the "how you say it" but light on the "what you say" was the Burger King advertising that featured the larger-than-life big-headed king. In the ads, this "Big King" kept popping up in surprising places, like on a football field – though probably anywhere a "Big King" would pop up would be surprising. What wasn't so clear was the compelling message for the brand. What made Burger King special? What was its competitive advantage versus McDonald's? Why should consumers care? This campaign was heavy on execution, and light on strategy.

Admittedly, not every brand has the inherent appeal of Viagra. Not every brand has the cool factor of Apple or Mini Cooper. But, you should search for the right message for your brand. What meaningful point of difference does your brand have? Why should someone choose your brand over your competitors?

There is nothing wrong with creativity in advertising – creativity can help a brand break through an incredibly cluttered communication environment. Creativity can be an important spark of life for a brand.

Creativity alone isn't a brand's compelling proposition.

Creativity alone, though, isn't sufficient to build a strong customer base. Creativity alone isn't a brand's compelling proposition. Creative advertising is great – but effective advertising is 90% what you say, 10% how you say it.

TRUTH

49

Compromise can destroy a brand

Brands are built on consistency – consistency of message, of image, of tone, of logo...the list goes on. Consistency does not happen overnight. It is developed through collaboration: collaboration between departments, with suppliers and vendors, with retailers, with all those who in any way touch or influence the brand. Everyone works together in a single-minded effort to connect the brand with your consumer. Compromising on even the smallest of details potentially begins an erosion that, once begun, can be difficult to stop.

Consider Boston Chicken. It was a very popular, fast-growing chain in the US that provided home-cooked chicken and meals – only it forgot what got it there. The company compromised on the brand: changing the name to Boston Market, extending its product offerings and identifying different locations from those that had originally worked. The result: brand erosion, fall off in sales, significant drops in earnings and stock price and, ultimately, bankruptcy.

> Compromising begins an erosion that, once begun, can be difficult to stop.

Compromise often feels like an easy answer. The pressure is on to drive sales and to increase share. The brand manager cannot possibly figure out how to gain additional sales in a competitive environment from the same target audience. So, "scope creep" – a slow gradual reduction in the focus of the brand – occurs. If you expand your target audience, if you express new elements of the brand, or if you team up with a brand that is not totally in sync with your brand values, perhaps you can squeeze out that additional share point. A little compromise goes a long way in brand destruction, as it leads to inconsistency and confusion in the marketplace. So, although the brand manager may, in fact, squeeze out a few additional share points, the long-term strength of the brand may have eroded a bit.

A bakery had a strong premium position in the marketplace. Its pricing reflected that position – it was clearly able to command a premium price because the consumer was enamoured with the quality of the product. In a meeting, the sales manager was excited because it was able to obtain a temporary price reduction that meant that for a week, it would be priced five cents below the closest competitor. The sales manager was thrilled, but shouldn't have been. That compromise on the brand's premium image might drive a few short-term sales, but what is its effect on the long-term sustainability of a well-regarded brand?

Compromising on price is a big red flag for brands. However, the little red flags can cause just as many problems. Many people believe that a small compromise here or there won't hurt much. However, the pain is two-fold. First of all, don't be mistaken – small compromises are noticed by the marketplace. Secondly, small compromises set the stage for compromise in general, which can damage the value of the brand.

Be vigilant on the little things. The smallest of elements can compromise a brand. Importantly, if you compromise on the small issues, you set the stage to allow compromises on the larger issues. A long-lasting battery may be communicated by a bunny that keeps going and going, except when the person in the bunny costume at an outdoor event gets tired and stops. The compromise of the message does not go unnoticed – a small example, but a compromise

Be vigilant on the little things.

nonetheless. How many small examples does it take before the brand's message is eroded? Why take the risk of finding out?

Collaboration, on the other hand, can help to enhance a brand. Collaborating with partners, ensuring that vendors, retailers and service providers all understand the nuance of the brand, can help eliminate unintentional compromise. It is so easy to keep the brand close to your chest – to consider vendors as vendors and not partners. However, all those who touch, support and drive your brand have the ability to compromise the brand unintentionally. "Collaborate, be transparent and ensure consistency" should be your operating style.

Successful brands require that constant vigilance. They require everyone to become supportive of the direction taken by the brand. They require everyone to be consistent in the communication of the message. Compromising on even the smallest of details can erode your brand's meaning. Collaboration focuses the team on building consistent meaning for your brand.

TRUTH

50

Don't let the pizazz outshine the brand

Marketers sometimes get so caught up in doing such fabulously creative marketing that they forget that the purpose of marketing is to communicate a message about a product or service. Many times, an ad campaign, a promotion or an event is so spectacular, it overshadows the brand it is supposed to be supporting.

In the US, Energizer battery marketers often used to look out the window, down the street, at Anheuser-Busch and remind themselves not to take the same road that the brewer took with Spuds Mackenzie. Spuds, a popular dog spokesman for the brewery giant, became so overexposed that he became ineffective. Spuds became an icon, a "cool" dog that was everywhere: a part of the advertising, in fabulous promotions, a hot stuffed toy...the list goes on. Unfortunately, Spuds overwhelmed the product he was supposed to represent, so Spuds had to go.

> The purpose of marketing is to communicate a message about a product or service.

Energizer was searching for a new promotion firm and went through the process of bringing five or six firms in to pitch. Each one had many fabulous ideas, but the ideas were all about the pink bunny mascot that the brand has used in the US since the 1980s (in Europe and Australia, rival Duracell uses a similar mascot). In a fit of exasperation, the director finally asked one firm, "Do you know what we sell?" The promotion agency responded, "Well, you sell batteries, but there are so many amazing things we can do with the bunny." The director shook her head and said, "We don't sell bunnies. Do something amazing for the battery." Fortunately, one firm came in and discussed the battery business; the bunny never came up. Guess who got the business? Yes, the bunny was used in its creative product, but it understood: the business was batteries.

Burger King has had a long history of problems, including disgruntled franchisees and a revolving door of senior executives. Burger King has run advertising with a slightly larger than life "king". This outsized symbol was developed into a video game character. With as many problems as Burger King has had in a highly competitive market, it would probably be better served focusing on tasty burgers and fries than on turning its advertising character into a video game.

Whether as a marketer you are using a character, a personality or some other creative engine to communicate your product or service's benefits, a most difficult task is staying on point – managing the brand to drive sales and profits. Unfortunately, marketers often get the accolades in their industry for their creative genius. It is hard to limit the creative genius when there are personal rewards to be attained. However, that very creative genius can frequently get in the way of the brand benefit communication.

Now, this isn't to say that pizazz is all bad. Not at all. It has a strong capability to engage and attract consumers, bring them into the brand franchise and generate interest and enthusiasm for the brand at hand. This is about understanding your fundamental objective.

The brands that have resonated over time and have shown consistent success are those that have practised moderation, even though spectacular opportunities abounded for them. Tony the Tiger and his communication of "They're grrrreat" could have been exploited in so many ways (alarm clocks that growl "They're grrrreat" at

> Creative genius can frequently get in the way of the product or service benefit communication.

the appointed time is just one example) that this iconic line would have worn out. It is the containment of that energy and the focus on Frosties that makes the brand strong year after year. True, there are web pages and YouTube commercials all linked to this famous tiger. But the pizazz of Tony doesn't get in the way of the message he communicates.

When you think of the brands that are strong year after year, most likely every single one of them has had the same conversation that occurred at Energizer. "Mr Brand Manager, do you know what we can do with those Keebler Elves?" "Do you have any idea how exciting we can make the Michelin Man?" "The idea of having the Jolly Green

Giant do____ (you name it) is as exciting as it gets." But, that is not the point. Characters, personalities and icons are simply tools in the brand manager's arsenal – important tools, but not the end game.

It is easy to get enamoured by an amazing character or a fabulous event. It is fun to be creative, and most marketers are always trying to "outdo" the previous manager. But, by doing that, you take the risk that the pizazz begins to overshadow the product. Most critical for the manager is the product or service. Keep your focus there and don't succumb to the excitement of pizazz.

TRUTH

51

There are no commodity products, only commodity thinking

Marketing managers commonly complain that they are in a commodity business. Products (or services) are functionally the same, they say. All that customers care about is price. Competition quickly copies our innovations, they complain.

Differentiation is the route out of a commodity business. Brands can differentiate in one of three ways – on physical attributes, service attributes and symbolic attributes. Differentiating on physical attributes comes most naturally to mind. Many brands rely heavily on this form of differentiation. Crocs sandals have become very popular. The sandals have a unique plastic design with distinctive openings throughout the sandal. Crest offers many variations on its toothpaste. You can buy Crest in traditional paste or, if you prefer, gel or liquid gel. You can get Crest with baking soda added.

Gillette introduced the Mach III shaving system in 1998. At the time, this three-blade razor was an innovative step forward – and a move by Gillette to differentiate its shaver on physical attributes (three blades instead of one or two). Key competitor Wilkinson Sword followed with its four-blade Quattro. And most recently, Gillette fired back with its five-blade Fusion. Competition on physical attributes.

Differentiation is the route out of a commodity business.

Water is commonly cited by economists as a great example of a commodity product. Yep, common H_2O. Dasani, a Coca-Cola brand, makes vitamin-enhanced variants claiming to cleanse and restore, defend and protect, or refresh and revive. Aquafina, a Pepsi product, starts out with regular tap water, adds some vitamins, some flavours, a nice package and creates a strong seller. You can get water bottled from Iceland (Iceland Springs), France (Perrier) and Canada (Penguin Ice). So much for water as a commodity.

Physical attributes are not the only way to distinguish a brand. Service and symbolic attributes can serve as effective differentiators. Service attributes include things such as warranty, after-sales support and financing options. Consider the brick – a hardened piece of clay. Is this a perfect example of a commodity? Not for Texas-based Acme

Brick Company. Although not the most distinctive of names, Acme bricks are backed by a confidence-inspiring 100-year warranty. Isuzu recently offered an industry-leading 7-year/75,000 mile transmission warranty to help differentiate its pickup trucks.

Service and symbolic attributes can serve as effective differentiators.

The US game shop Great Hall Games competes against online retailers by creating a local community of gamers with regular events. Although the games it sells can be found on websites, the welcoming environment and game-friendly facilities cannot be duplicated over a computer. Starbucks sells coffee. It's fancy coffee. It's expensive coffee – but it is coffee. Starbucks has taken this basic commodity and wrapped it within a cosy, inviting ambiance staffed by knowledgeable baristas. No commodity thinking here.

Symbolic attribute differentiation is differentiation developed around brand image. Consider the highly competitive soft drink category. Fizzy cola is basically carbonated sugar water. Success in this market is less about warranties and ingredients and more about image. Coca-Cola is a more traditional brand infused with the spirit of American life. Pepsi-Cola has differentiated itself on a more youthful image. Dr Pepper has been a bit more of a wacky, off-beat brand. What about RC Cola and Shasta? No strong image – no symbolic differentiation.

Vodka is one of the most basic of distilled spirits. Although there are a number of vodkas infused with assorted flavours, much vodka is sold in its virgin state. Vodka producers turn to symbolic differentiation, imagery, to sell their brands. You can get vodka associated with a great musician (Chopin) or a great artist (Van Gogh). You can buy vodka named after a place (Finlandia) or ancient warriors (Vikingfjord) or one that evokes the space race of the 1960s (Sputnik). These vodkas compete not on taste, but on imagery.

Colognes and perfumes are marketed primarily on symbolic imagery. Although there are certainly some physical differences here and there with the scents, the real marketing power comes from the imagery created around the brands. Cool Water by Davidoff evokes imagery of refreshing tranquility. Stetson cologne promises the "legendary fragrance of the American West". No idea what the American West actually smells like – it's the imagery it is selling. Ralph Lauren's Polo Black evokes a sophisticated urban sense, whereas the promotional ad for Ralph Lauren's Safari features imagery of rugged men in khakis, helicopters, vintage 4×4s and a tough desert environment. Symbolic differentiation in action.

Agricultural products are commonly considered commodities. Yet companies and industry trade groups have succeeded in creating brands – brands that have transcended the ordinary inherent in their business. Sunkist oranges, Del Monte pineapple, Jersey Royal potatoes and Washington apples have all created a positive distinction based on branding.

Colombia is fertile coffee-growing territory. Coffee, like oranges, pineapples, potatoes and apples, is a basic agricultural staple. The National Federation of Coffee Growers of Colombia built symbolic distinction into its brand through the use of Juan Valdez. Sporting a moustache, sombrero and with his ever-present donkey, this icon became a symbol representing the quality of 100% Colombian coffee.

Do you consider your brand to be competing in an undifferentiated commodity market? Have you not created your brand's unique distinction? There are no commodity products – only commodity thinking.

References

Truth 3

Ind, Nicholas. *Living the Brand: How to Transform Every Member of Your Organization into the Brand Champion.* Kogan Page, 2001.

Truth 4

Hindo, Brian. "Monsanto: Winning the Ground War; How the Company Turned the Tide in the Battle over Genetically Modified Crops." *Business Week*, Dec. 17, 2007, p. 34.

Truth 5

Aaker, David A., and Erich Joachimsthaler. *Brand Leadership.* The Free Press, 2000.

Truth 6

Davis, Scott. *Brand Asset Management: Driving Profitable Growth Through Your Brands.* Jossey-Bass, Inc., 2000.

Truth 7

Travis, Daryl. *Emotional Branding.* Prima Publishing, 2000.

Truth 9

Williams, Roy, H. *Wizards of Ads.* Capstone, 1999.

Truth 11

Aaker, David A., and Erich Joachimsthaler. *Brand Leadership.* The Free Press, 2000.

Truth 16

Ind, Nicholas. *Living the Brand: How to Transform Every Member of Your Organization into the Brand Champion.* Kogan Page, 2001.

Truth 17

Davis, Scott. *Brand Asset Management: Driving Profitable Growth Through Your Brands.* Jossey-Bass, Inc., 2000.

Laverty, Kevin J. "Market Share, Profits, and Business Strategy." Management Decision, Vol. 39 (8), 2001, pp. 607–617.

Miniter, Richard. *The Myth of Market Share: Why Market Share is the Fool's Gold of Business.* Crown Business, 2002.

Truth 20

Adamson, Allen P. *Brand Simple: How the Best Brands Keep It Simple and Succeed.* Palgrave Macmillan, 2006.

Truth 21

Reis, Al, and Trout, Jack. *Marketing Warfare.* McGraw-Hill, 2005.

Truth 22

Markey, Rob, John Ott and Gerard du Toit. "Winning New Customers Using Loyalty-Based Segmentation." *Strategy & Leadership*, Vol. 35 (3), 2007, pp. 32–37.

Ries, Al. *Focus: The Future of Your Company Depends on It.* HarperBusiness, 1996.

Truth 25

Trout, Jack. *Differentiate or Die: Survival in Our Era of Killer Competition.* John Wiley & Sons, 2000.

Trout, Jack. *Trout on Strategy.* McGraw-Hill, 2004.

Truth 26

Ries, Al, and Jack Trout. *Positioning: The Battle for Your Mind.* McGraw-Hill, 2001.

Truth 27

Reichheld, Frederick R. *Loyalty Rules: How Today's Leaders Build Lasting Relationships.* Harvard Business School Publishing, 2001.

Truth 29

Till, Brian D., and Michael Busler. "The Match-Up Hypothesis: Physical Attraction, Expertise, and the Role of Fit on Brand Attitude, Purchase Intent, and Brand Beliefs." *Journal of Advertising*, Vol. 29 (3), pp. 1–13.

Zafer, Erdogan B., Michael J. Baker and Stephen Tagg. "Selecting Celebrity Endorsers: The Practitioner's Perspective." *Journal of Advertising Research*, Vol. 41 (3), 2001, pp. 39–48.

Truth 31

McWilliams, Jeremiah. "It's Super Sunday for Advertising and Bud Brands Are Set for Kickoff, Too." *St. Louis Post-Dispatch*, Jan. 22, 2008, p. C9.

Truth 35

Adamson, Allen P. *Brand Simple: How the Best Brands Keep It Simple and Succeed.* Palgrave Macmillan, 2006.

Truth 36

Ries, Al, and Jack Trout. *Positioning: The Battle for Your Mind.* McGraw-Hill, 2001.

Truth 38

Aaker, David A. *Managing Brand Equity: Capitalizing on the Value of a Brand Name.* The Free Press, 1991.

Trout, Jack. *Differentiate or Die: Survival in Our Era of Killer Competition.* John Wiley & Sons, 2000.

Truth 42

Ries, Al, and Jack Trout. *The 22 Immutable Laws of Marketing.* HarperBusiness, 1993.

Truth 43

Sullivan, Luke. *Hey Whipple, Squeeze This.* John Wiley & Sons, 2008.

Truth 44

We are grateful to our colleague, Ken Stern, for this wonderful line – "It's a Long Walk from the Focus Group Room to the Cash Register."

Truth 46

"Can VW Finally Find Its Way in America?" *Business Week.* July 23, 2007, p. 31.

Seiden, Hank. *Advertising Pure and Simple.* AMACOM, 1990.

Truth 49

See *Hitting the Sweet Spot,* by Lisa Fortini-Campbell (The Copy Workshop, 2001), for a great discussion on the difference between compromise and collaboration.

Acknowledgements

We would like to express our thanks to Jennifer Simon at Pearson Education for her support and strategic guidance with this book. Also, thanks to Russ Hall, whose editing suggestions and advice sharpened both our ideas and our writing. We also appreciate the early advice of Scottie Priesmeyer on the rewards and challenges of writing and publishing.

We extend our sincere appreciation to our colleagues with whom we have worked closely, and studied from, at great companies and universities. Interactions with the wonderful people at organisations such as Campbell-Mithun, DePauw University, Energizer Battery, Indiana University, Monsanto, Prophet, Ralston Purina, University of South Carolina and the University of Texas at Austin have shaped and influenced our thinking over the years. Specifically, we'd like to acknowledge the following individuals who have been particularly rewarding to work with and have engaged us in great conversations about marketing strategy and branding: Dr David Aaker, Dr Dan Baack, Steve Burkhardt, Bob Graham, Mark Halton, Tom Hayden, Dr Tom Hustad, Jay Milliken, Bob Morrison, Kevin O'Donnell, Maurice Parisien, Andy Pierce, Dr Terry Shimp, Laurie Steam, Ken Stern and Susan Widham.

About the authors

Dr Brian D. Till is the Steber Professor of Marketing and Chair of the Marketing Department at Saint Louis University. He holds a BS in Advertising and an MBA from the University of Texas at Austin. His PhD is from the University of South Carolina. At Saint Louis University, he teaches primarily marketing strategy and advertising courses to MBA students. His research is in the areas of celebrity endorsements, associative learning and brand equity. He has published in *Journal of Advertising, Journal of Advertising Research, Journal of Marketing Research, Journal of the Academy of Marketing Science, Journal of Consumer Marketing, Journal of Current Issues and Research in Advertising, Sport Marketing Quarterly, Journal of Product & Brand Management* and *Psychology & Marketing.* Dr Till serves on the editorial review boards of *Journal of Advertising* and *Psychology & Marketing.*

Prior to his university career, Dr Till worked in brand management at Purina. He continues to serve as a marketing strategy and advertising consultant. Previous clients include Energizer, Monsanto, AT&T, Boa Construction, Charter Communication, Concordia Publishing House, Squeaky Clean Car Wash and Medicine Shoppe International. He is active in the community, with recent nonprofit board appointments with the Stella Maris Child Center (where he recently completed four years as board president) and Forest ReLeaf of Missouri. Dr Till is also a founding principal of the Brand Cartography Group, a market research firm that specialises in research designed to provide strategic insight into the structure of brands.

Dr Till is single, and in his free time enjoys travel, his historic home and outdoor activities such as running, flying and motorcycle riding.

Donna Heckler is the Brand Strategy Lead for Monsanto, where she leads the company in its brand building and brand portfolio management. Ms Heckler has a BA in Zoology from DePauw University and an MBA in Marketing from Indiana University.

Ms Heckler has provided strategic brand guidance for a variety of firms. She has worked for Energizer Batteries to lead brand efforts both domestically and internationally. She led the brand marketing domestically and internationally for a division of Cardinal Health. She also led brand activities for Kimball Office.

Ms Heckler had a brand strategy consulting firm for a number of years, where she supported such clients as The Clorox Company, Emerson Electric, Maritz, Inc., The American Red Cross and Ralston Purina.

Ms Heckler is actively involved in the community and supports a number of art institutions. She currently serves on the Alumni Board for the Kelley School of Business at Indiana University. She is a board member for the Center for Brand Leadership and The International Institute of Greater St Louis. She also sits on the Alumni Board for Indiana University.

Ms Heckler loves travelling, experiencing new cultures and art. An avid animal lover, she lives with two cats – Honey and Muffin.